Thank you for buying this coloring book.

Anna and I created this book in honor of our beloved pup, Kiko, that recently passed due to health complications. She was very young and full of life but sometimes things happen unexpectedly and there is nothing that we can do, except to continue to love.

Love was all that Kiko cared about. Except for eating a fresh carrot!

Anna and I also used the time creating this book to help us to heal. We wanted to share it with everyone because the love that Kiko shared with us, still burns fiercely in our hearts, so much so, that we cannot contain it all.

Please enjoy Kiko's coloring book and remember to show those that you love how much they mean to you.

Aloha pumehana,

Anna and Roland

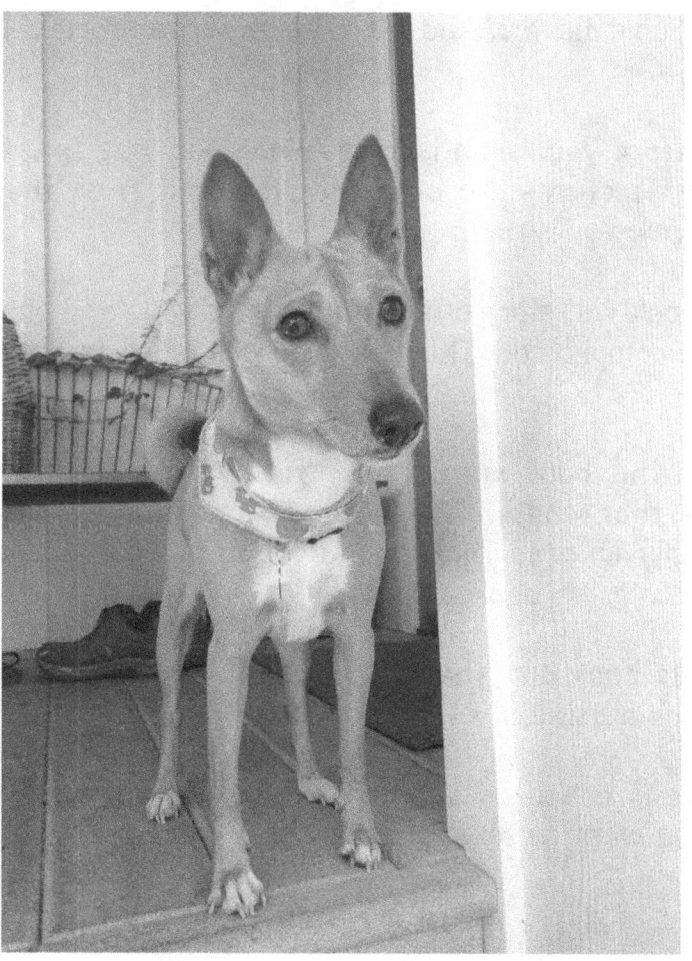

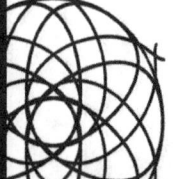
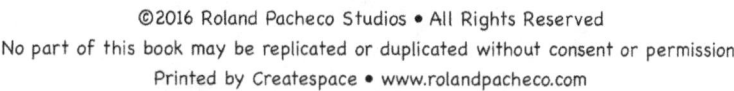
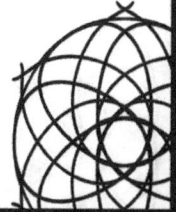

PLEASE TAKE TIME TO READ THIS

If you have any trouble reading all of this, just ask an adult to help you!

Anna is a professional photographer, which means that she takes pictures with a fancy camera. She also loves all animals, especially dogs. She loves nothing more than to take pictures of dogs. She is really good at that.

Anna doesn't only take fabulous pictures, she can draw too. The only thing is that she doesn't think she's very good at drawing. Not as good as she is at taking pictures. But even though drawing isn't her biggest strength, she does it anyway because she wants to get better. The only way you can get better at anything, from eating cheeseburgers to flying an airplane, is to practice and try to do your best.

Roland is a professional tattoo artist. That means that he draws permanent pictures on people for a living. Which is good because he couldn't take a picture if it had handles on it!

He loves all dogs and animals too. And he likes to write stories, like the one you are about to read.

Something to know before you begin is that Anna's job was to draw Kiko and some of her things. All of these pictures are bold and stand out from the rest of the picture. Roland pretty much drew everything else.

The drawings in this book will start out simply, but as you read on, the story and drawings will become more complicated. This is so you can learn to familiarize yourself with details.

All of the drawings in this book are done in "flash" style. A tattoo artist will draw up a design for someone that wants a tattoo and that drawing is called flash. Because flash is made up of only lines so that the tattoo artist can add colors as they work, flash is perfect for a coloring book.

Remember, this is your book and there is no right or wrong way to color it. You can color inside the lines or outside, it's up to you!

The flash in this book is based on Japanese style art, so there are a few things to know about that if you want to do it properly.

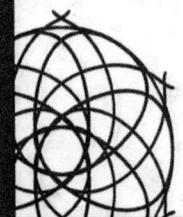
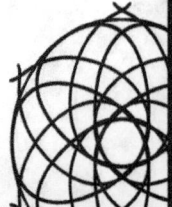

Wind and Water bars

These lines are found in the background of the drawings and are used to give a sense of motion by including clouds, waves, stars and wind. The proper way to use the lines are to shade the lines upward being careful to fade out before it reaches the line above it.

Here is an example:

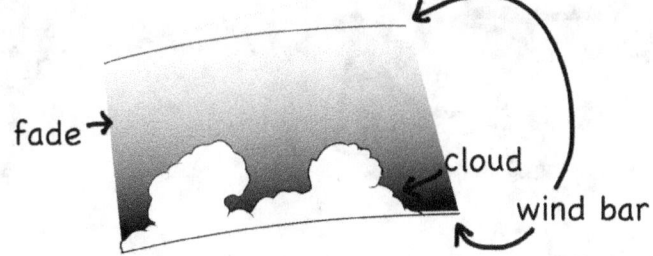

Again, you don't have to do it this way, you could color them solid, it doesn't matter!

Waves and water

Waves and water tend not to be colored solidly and many times the color or shading of the wave will fade out before the edge so that it creates an illusion of white caps.

Here is an example:

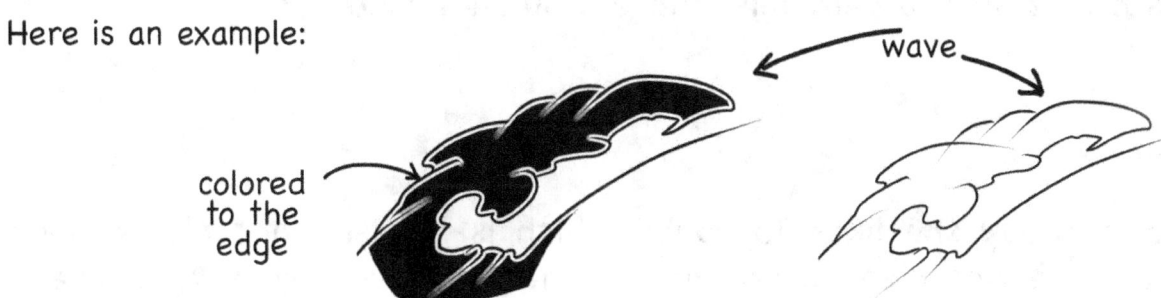

It's also highly recommended that you use colored pencils or crayons for this book. Any ink based color could bleed through the page and onto the artwork behind it. This is why it is also recommended that you read the entire book before you start coloring, so that you don't miss out on the adventure.

There is a lot of detail in all of these drawings so make sure you take the time to look at all of it before you begin coloring so that you don't miss a thing!

Now, help Kiko find a sunshine patch and remember to take your time so that you can get to know her too!

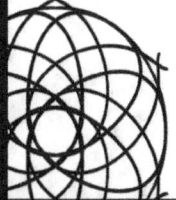
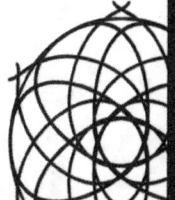

Please Note!
If you do decide to use ink based pens,
place a sheet or two of paper, or a thin piece of
cardboard under the page that you are working on.
This will keep the ink from ruining the artwork
on the following page!

This is Kiko.

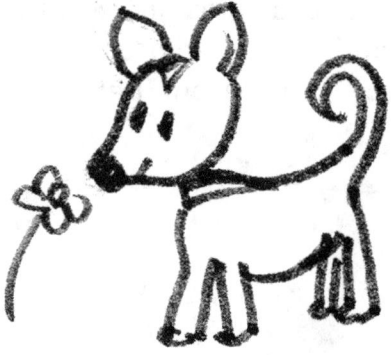

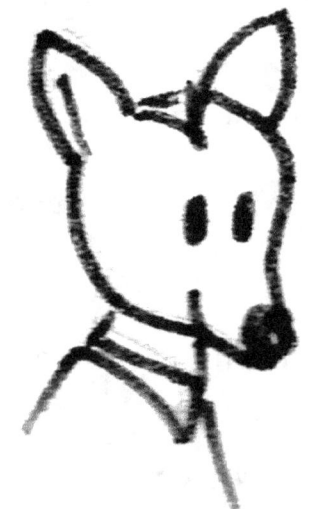

She is a very special dog in many ways.

For one thing, she is a Basenji.

She has pointy ears and a curly tail and she hardly ever makes a sound. Most dogs are noisy and very misbehaved, but not Kiko.

When she is happy she likes to yodel, which is like singing only without using words. She was also raised with manners and is always very sweet and kind to others.

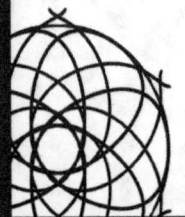

Kiko is a great explorer and always loves a good adventure. She loves the sunshine and spends most of her time trying to find a nice place to lay down and enjoy the beauty of her surroundings.

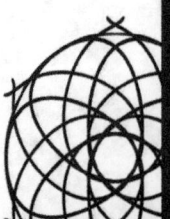

On this particular day, Kiko knew that big adventures were going to happen. But because Kiko was always on a big adventure, today she was a bit tired. She wanted nothing more than to go on a big adventure, but at the same time, all she wanted to do was to find a nice place to lay down and enjoy the warm sun on her belly.

Because Kiko was raised with manners she knew that it would be rude to just fall asleep anywhere, like all the dirty and stinky dogs do. She knew that she had to find the perfect place to lay down so that she could enjoy the day.

So, Kiko packed up her exploring gear and headed off down the road. She had heard of a frog that lived in a swamp and was hoping that the frog would help her find a nice place to lay down and get some sun on her belly.

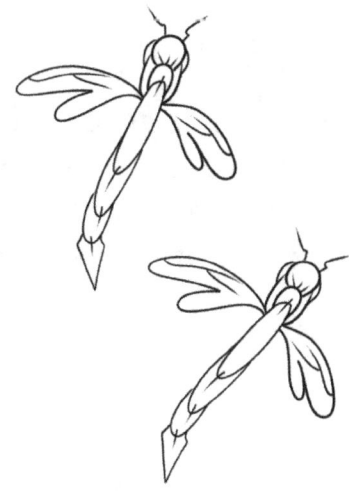

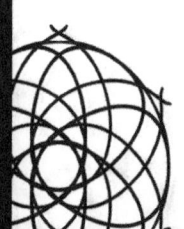

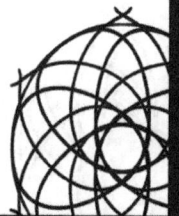

When Kiko arrived at the swamp the first thing that she noticed was that everything was wet. The ground was wet, the plants were wet and even the air was wet! There was hardly any sunshine poking through the clouds and the sky was dark and gray.

There were bugs flying around and the smell of rotten eggs hung in the air. But because she was well groomed and raised with manners, she did not let any of those things bother her.

She searched every pond and stick until she found the swamp frog, sitting proud on a lily pad. She introduced herself, like any proper puppy should, so that the swamp frog would know that she was friendly and well be-haved.

"Hello, Mister swamp frog," she said. "How are you doing on this fine day?"

The swamp frog burped and a dragonfly flew out of his mouth. Kiko noticed that the swamp frog was very slimy and had very bad breath. He moved slowly and watched every move that she made with his beady little eyes.

"I'm not feeling well," said the swamp frog. " I have had terrible indiges-tion lately and can't seem to keep any food down. I think I might have a gluten allergy or maybe I just need to exercise more, I don't know. But the real question is: what are you doing in my swamp?"

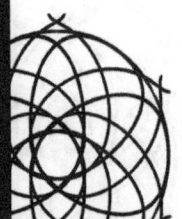
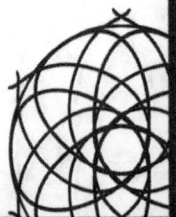

Kiko knew then that the frog was very rude and possessive, but because she had manners and was polite to all creatures, she knew that she shouldn't tell him so.

"Well, I am looking for a nice place to lay down and let the sun warm my belly," she replied.

"Pish posh!" said the frog. "There is no such place like that around here! The swamp is cold, wet, stinky and full of slimy creatures. This is not a place for a puppy."

Kiko nodded because she had already figured this out.

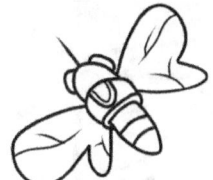

"Go talk to the flying crane," swamp frog said. "She lives over in the bamboo forest. She might be able to help you find this place because she is always flying up so high."

Kiko thought this was a good idea. She was also convinced that the frog did not have Celiac disease and was simply being melodramatic. So, she thanked the swamp frog and headed for the bamboo forest.

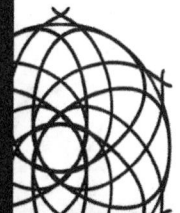
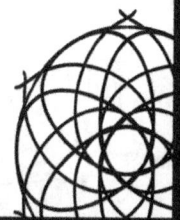

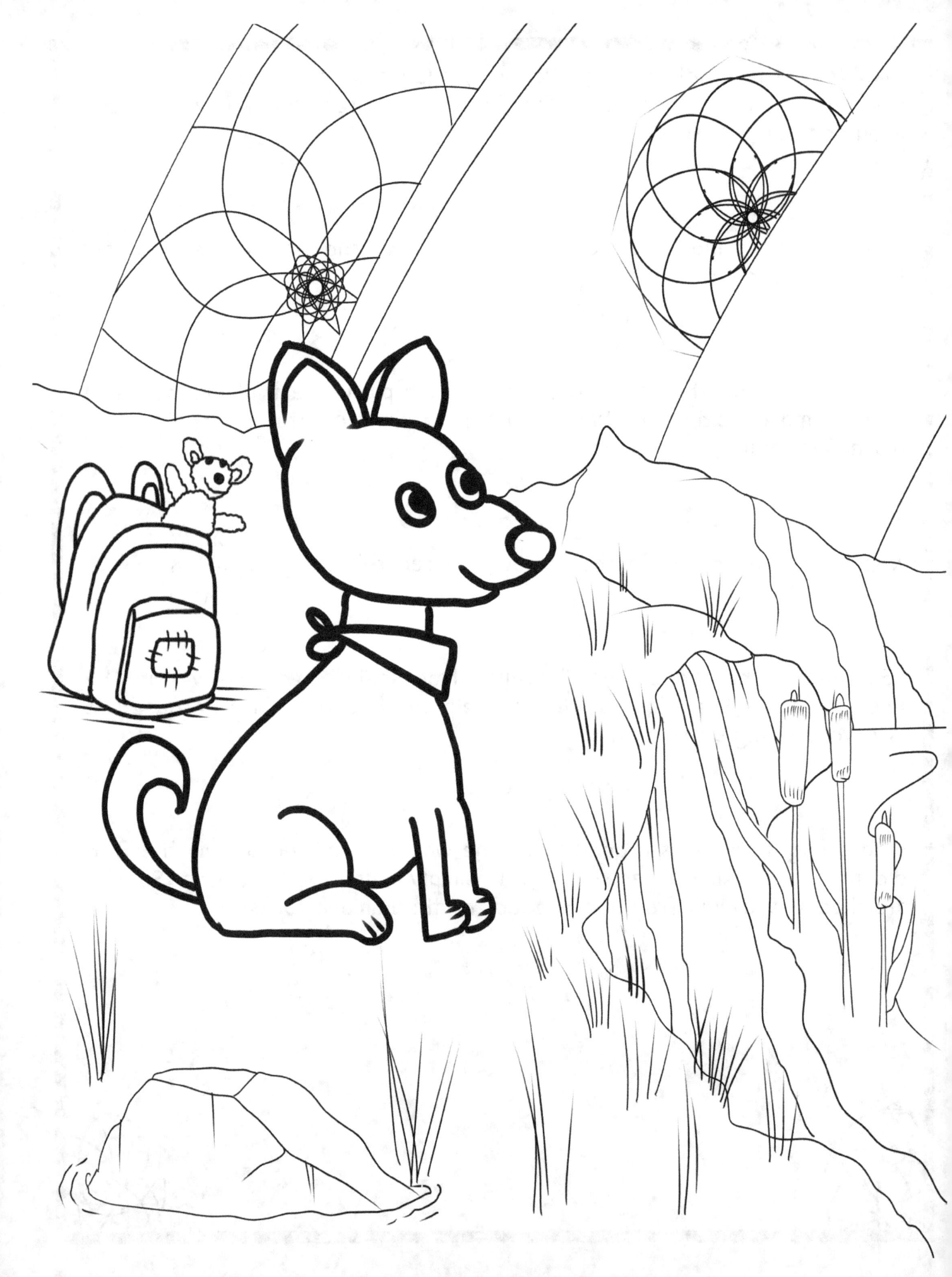

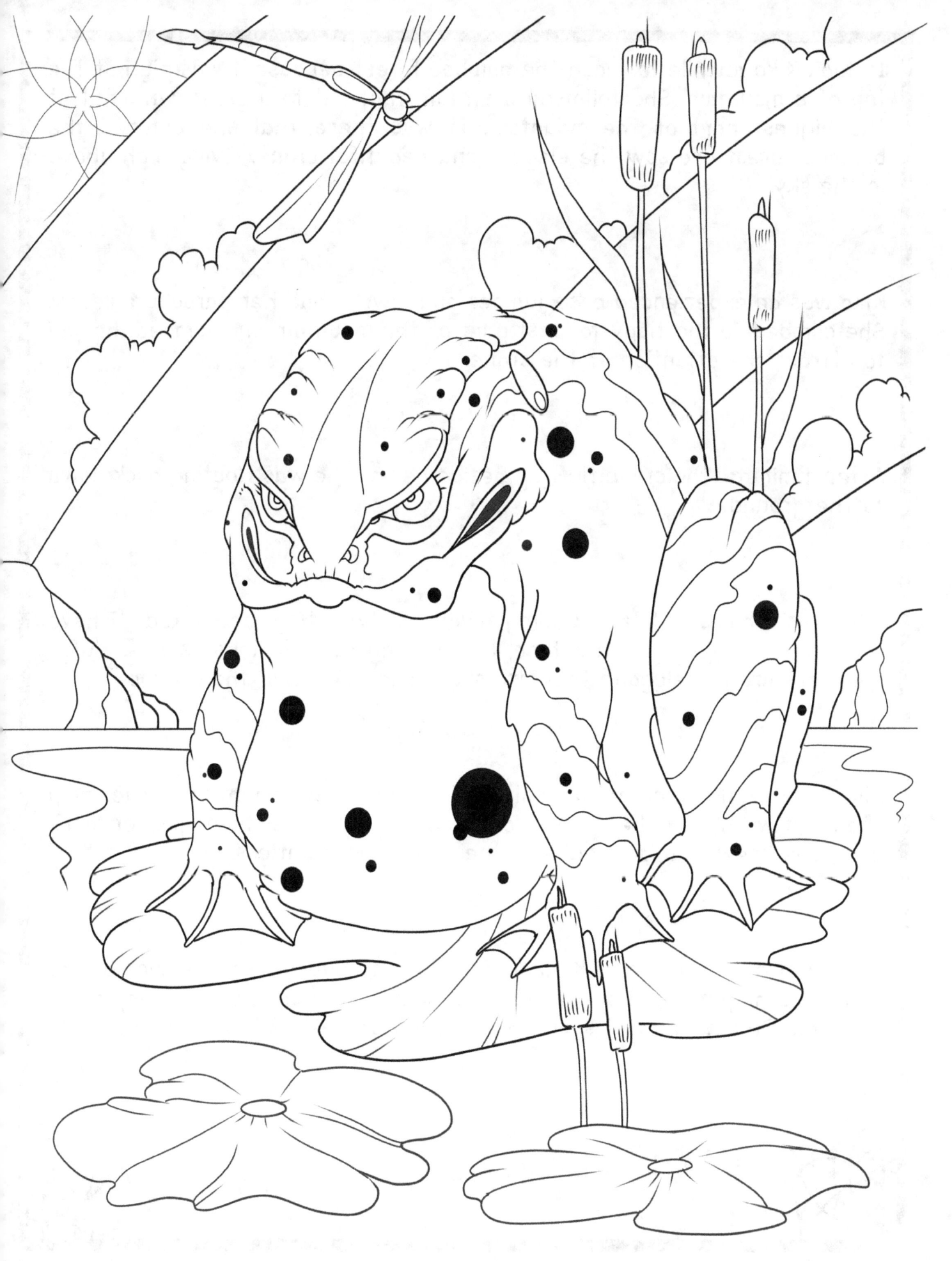

It took Kiko a while to reach the bamboo forest because it was high at the top of a mountain. She followed a stream that led to a giant waterfall at the highest part of the mountain. It was there that she entered the bamboo forest and saw the elegant and beautiful crane, flying high above in the sky.

Kiko was an experienced base jumper and always had her parachute ready. She climbed to the tippy toppest part of the mountain and jumped, hoping to attract the attention of the crane.

After a minute, the crane flew up beside her as she was floating back down to the ground.

"What is a hamster like you doing trying to fly?" the crane asked. "I have seen many things in my life time, but nothing as ridiculous as this. Fluffy hamsters are not elegant, they are short and belong on the ground."

Kiko knew that the crane was only saying what she thought was true, even though it wasn't. And because Kiko had strong self esteem and proper manners, she knew that arguing with the crane was pointless.

"I am not a hamster," said Kiko. "I am a basenji puppy and was hoping that you could help me find a nice warm sunshine patch so that I can lay down and rest. Do you know of such a place, Miss Crane?"

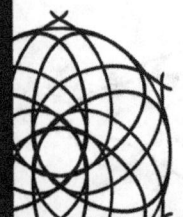
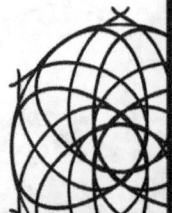

"Hoo hah!" said the crane. "I hardly ever come down from the sky and when I do, I go to my nest that is high up in the trees. The sunshine is always out to warm my feathers, but I can tell you that a nest is no place for a basenji puppy. If that is even what you are."

Kiko laughed.

"That is exactly what I am," she said. "I have been a basenji puppy all of my life. And I know now that I cannot find a sunshine patch up here. Have you seen any such places on your adventures, Miss Crane? I really want to find a place to warm my belly."

The crane thought about it for a moment and then said, "Go to the temple and ask the Foo dog. He is a little crazy and is on a strict vegan diet, but he is also very well traveled and might be able to help you."

Kiko had never heard of a foo dog before but was certain that they would get along well, since they were both canines.

She thanked the crane and floated down in the direction of the temple.

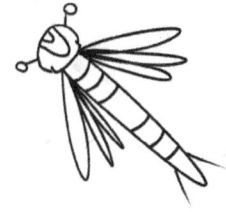

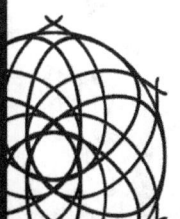

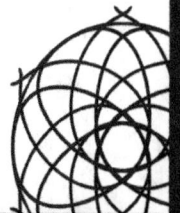

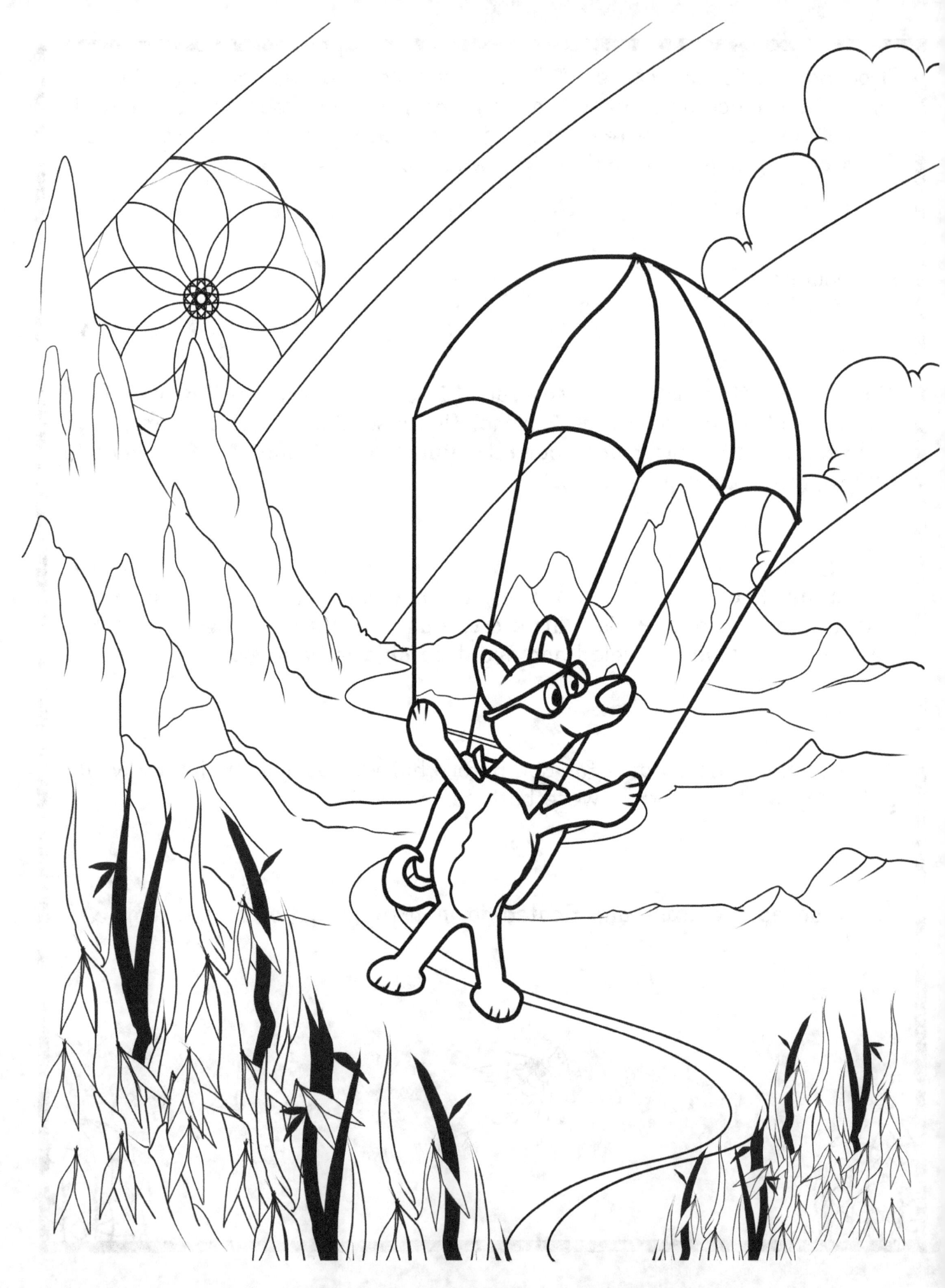

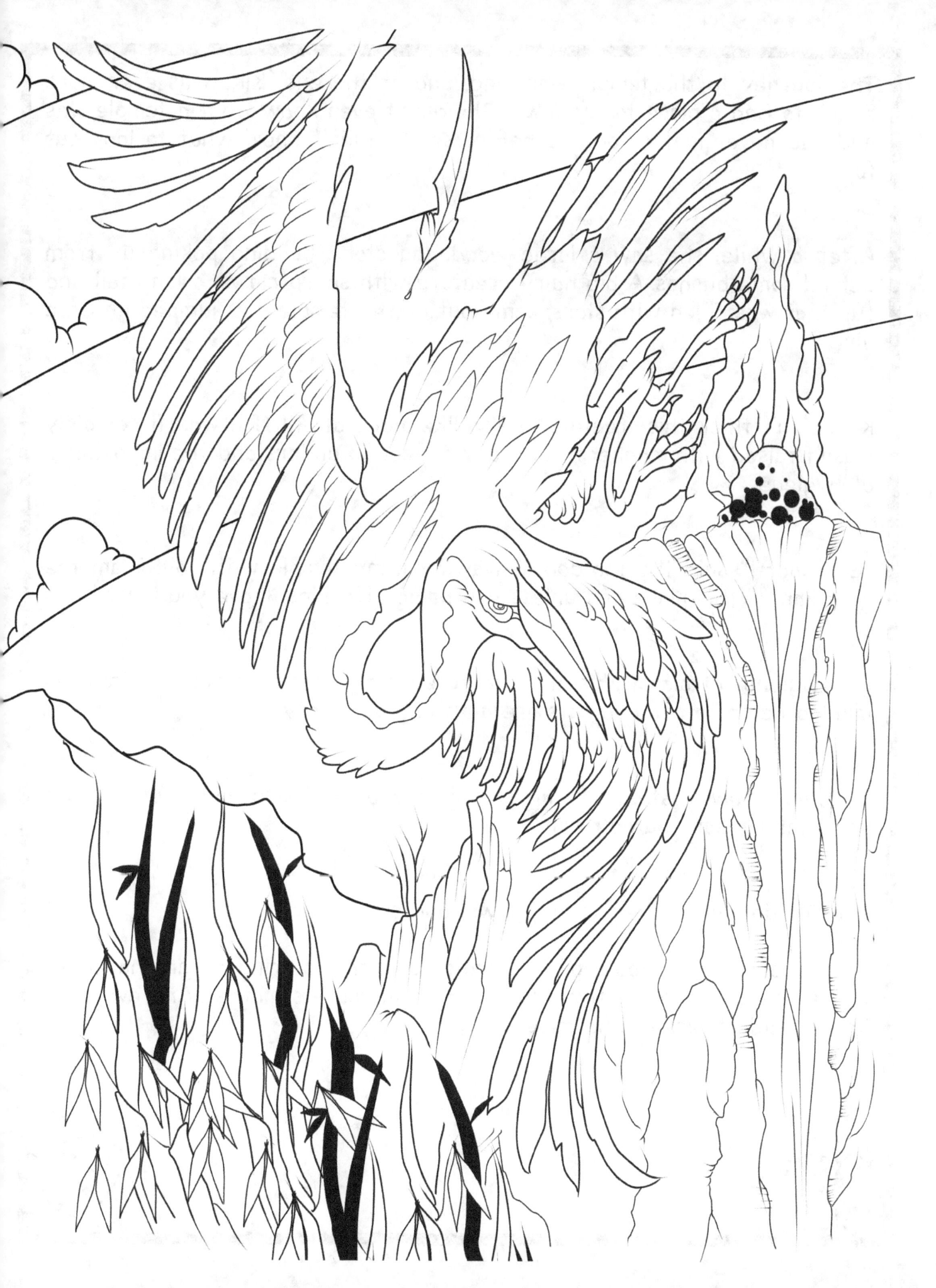

The journey to the temple was long, and at the end, Kiko was ever more eager to find a place to lay down. She didn't even know what a temple was and had never met a foo dog before so she didn't know what to look out for.

After a while, she saw a large wood and stone building poking up from behind some bushes. A big hairy creature with sharp claws, a long tail and fur that was filled with stars, came out of the temple and jumped into the air.

Kiko didn't think this creature looked like a dog at all! If it was, it certainly wasn't raised with manners, nor did it appear to understand the importance of hygiene.

"Grrrooooff!" said the foo dog. "Away from my temple with you! I am the guardian of this place and unless you bring offerings, leave you must."

Kiko was not afraid of this menacing creature, in fact, his crazy hairdo reminded her of a cat, and cats are anything but scary.

"I do not know what an offering is, mighty foo dog," Kiko said. "But I assure you that I mean you no harm."

The Foo dog looked her up and down, and side to side.

"'tis true," said the Foo dog. "You could not mean to bring me any harm because you are simply a stray kitten that has lost its mother. And everyone knows that kittens are harmless."

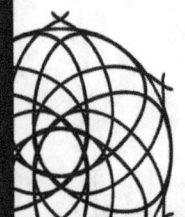
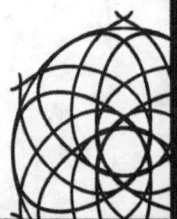

Kiko thought for a moment. "I am not a kitten, mighty foo dog, I am a basenji. And so that makes me a dog".

"A dog?" laughed the foo dog. "Impossible! For I am a mighty dog and we look nothing alike. You are short and have pointy ears and a curly tail, while I have a big mane, sharp claws and a love for grilled cheese sandwiches. Also, I will pee in a corner of the room that you will never be able to find."

Kiko considered his words.

"Well sir, not meaning to offend, but we don't have to look exactly alike to be the same," Kiko said. "But I'm quite sure that you are not a dog. You are some kind of cat or otherwise sneaky creature. By the way, aren't you vegan?"

The foo dog twisted in the air, his shiny mane that was filled with stars reminded Kiko of the sky at night.

"Vegan? How dare you insult my bad memory!" roared the foo dog. "If you bring me no sandwiches, then you must leave at once, lest I scratch you up like a new leather couch and then cough hair balls into your favorite pair of shoes."

Kiko did not know what to say to the crazy foo dog, but she now knew that a steady diet of grilled cheese sandwiches was probably not such a good thing. She also knew that the foo dog would be of no help to her since he could barely keep up with the conversation. So, like any polite puppy would, she thanked him for his time and made her way down the road.

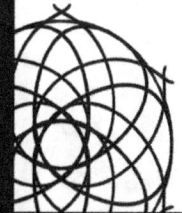

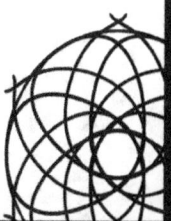

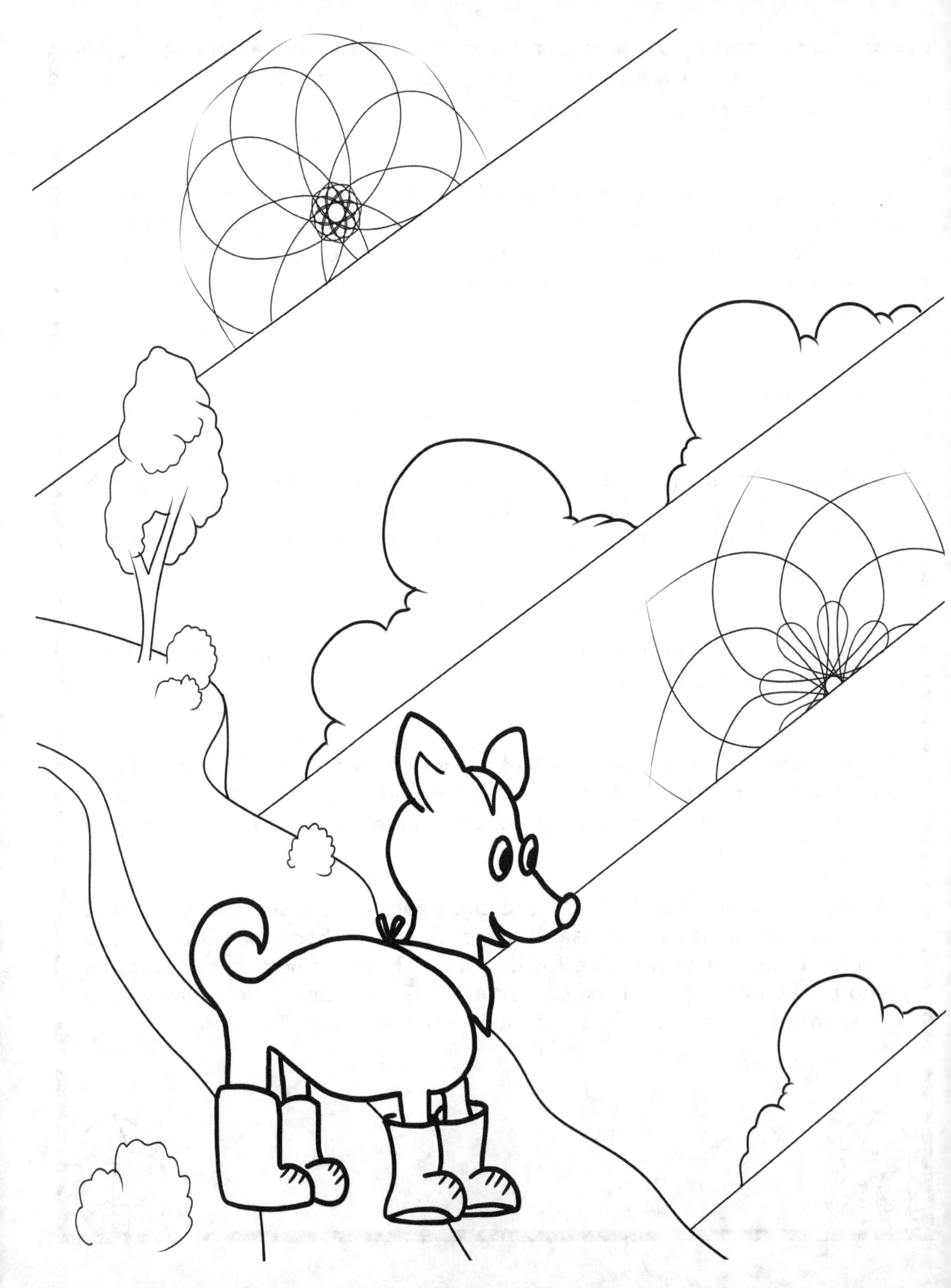

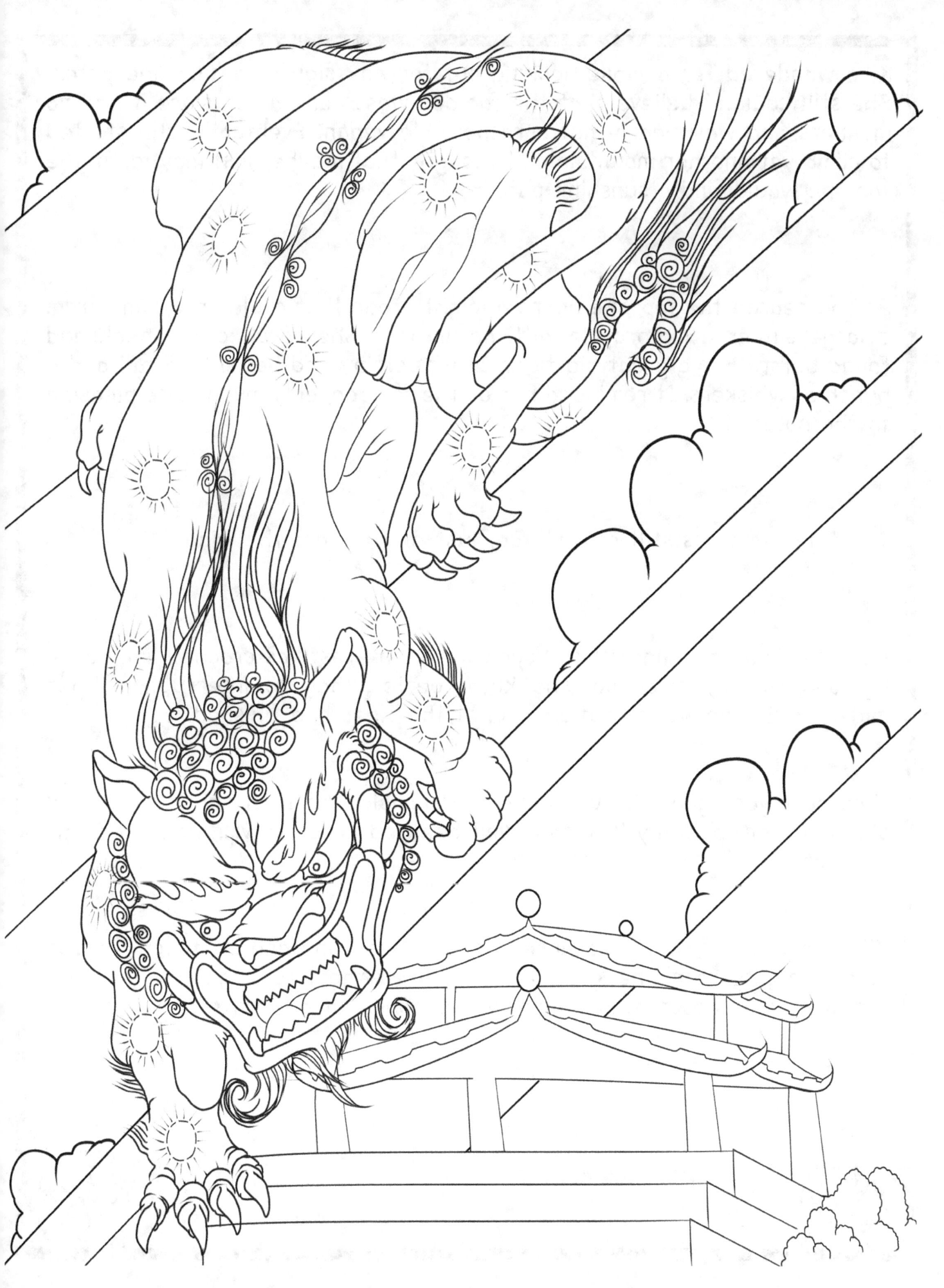

Kiko wandered for a while, looking out for any sign of a sunshine patch. She still couldn't believe that the foo dog was really a dog since it had no manners and was clearly not a responsible vegan. Eventually, she started to climb yet another mountain and thought that maybe, just maybe, at the top she would find a sunshine patch.

As she neared the top, she heard a mighty roar that could only come from a large cat or a motorcycle with no muffler. She reached the peak and found before her a great big tiger. It was stripy and had a long tail and a bunch of whiskers. It reminded her of the foo dog, only much more pleasing to the nose.

The tiger stood as still as a statue, just roaring into the wind.

Because Kiko had manners and such varied interests as crochet, line dancing and runway modeling, she knew better than to interrupt a tiger mid-roar. So she waited patiently until the tiger had finished.

"You have very good posture for a dog animal," the tiger said after it had stopped roaring. "Why is such a well behaved creature visiting me on this exquisite day?"

Kiko cleared her throat because her voice was tiny and no match for the tiger's mighty roar. She knew that she liked the tiger right away; if not for her astute observation, then for her choice of adjectives.

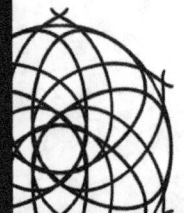
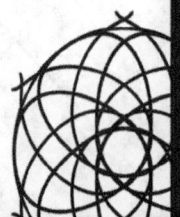

"I am searching for a sunshine patch, somewhere that I can warm my belly and relax." Kiko said. "Is this such a place?"

"Well," the tiger began. "It certainly is for me. As you can see, I rather enjoy a day filled with roaring and looking menacing yet approachable, on the top of this mountain. Sometimes the sun comes out and sometimes it is gloomy and cold. Either way, it does not matter, because I look magnificent and slim in the belly area, just the same."

Kiko knew that the tiger must be right. To stand upon a mountaintop every day, just to roar, meant that the tiger had no access to cable television or any board games.

"If you are looking for a sunny place to warm yourself, I would suggest going further towards the ice, where the days are as long as the nights." said the tiger. "I notice that you are also having a minor pizza problem, you should have that looked at. Now if you'll excuse me, I have to mark my territory."

Kiko listened to the tiger as the mighty beast roared into the wind, and then gingerly made her way back down the mountain.

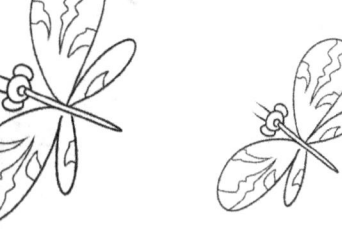

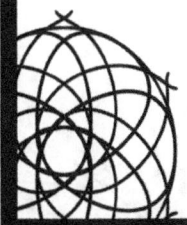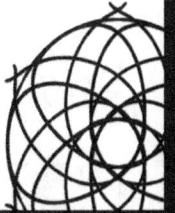

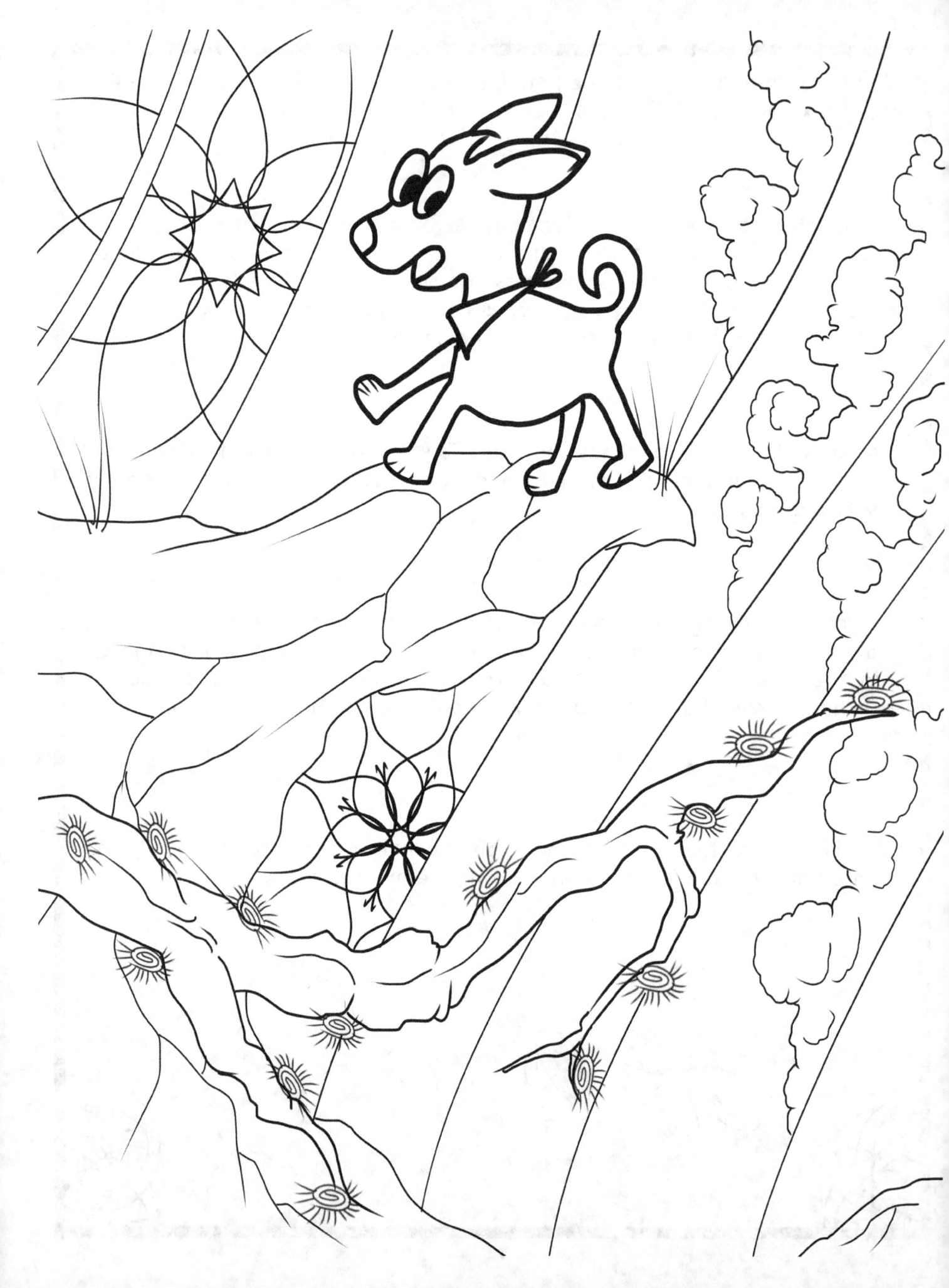

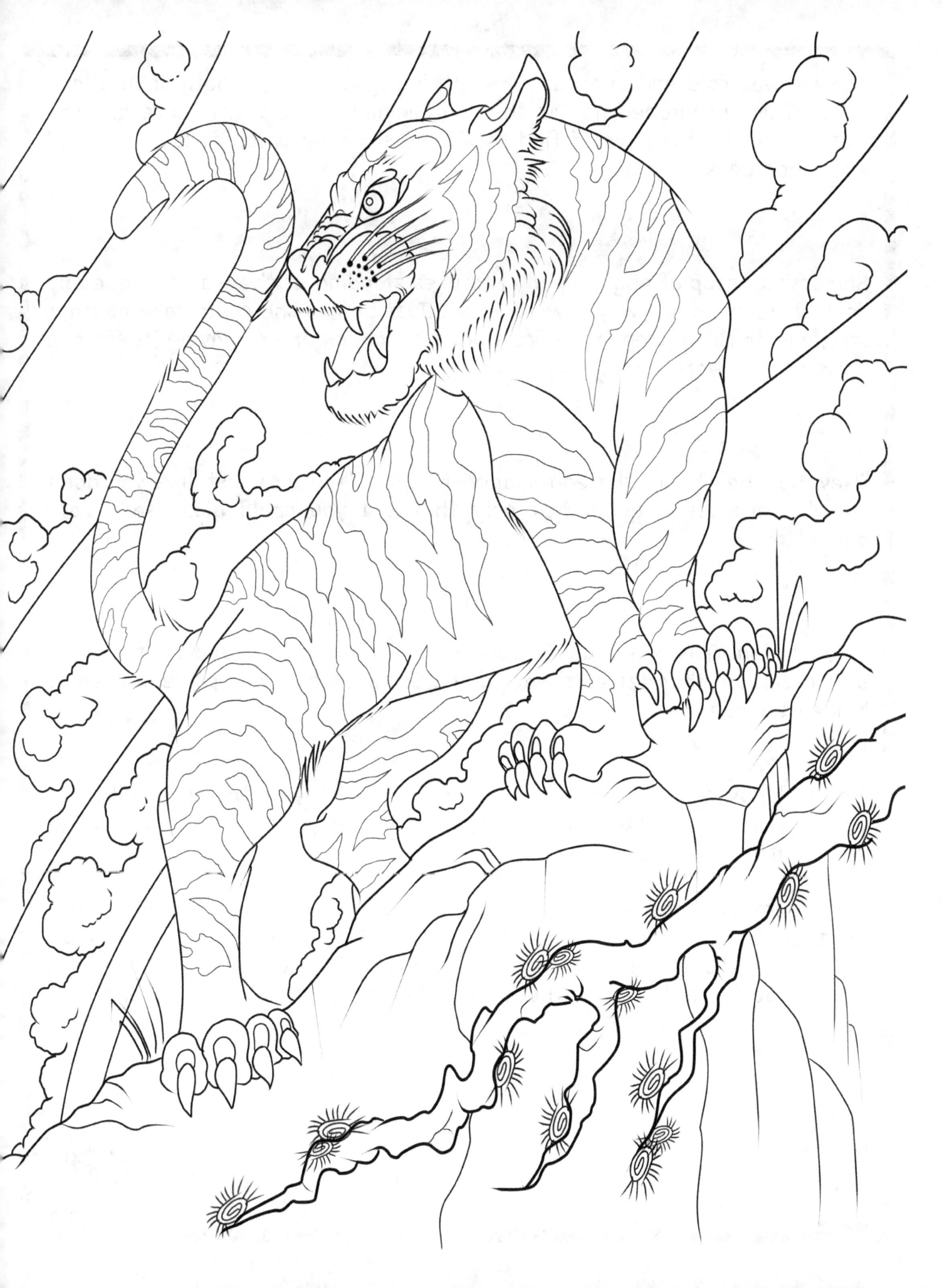

The air was cold and crisp and everything looked very bright, in the land of ice. This encouraged her as the sun seemed to be everywhere and she was certain that she would find a suitable sunshine patch to lay down and warm her belly.

She saw a group of egg-shaped creatures standing at the water's edge and decided to make her way toward them. Just before she could take another step, one of them jumped out from behind a chunk of ice, waving its strange arms as if it were trying to fly.

"Hey, hey, hey!" said the egg-shaped flapper. "You look lost, like you don't know where you're going. Not only that, but you could also use a bath behind the ears."

Kiko nodded. This was true. But she was also quite offended by the egg's bold assertion that her ears were dirty. She took care and pride in keeping her ears clean.

"Well, flappy egg," she said. "You are correct by saying that I do not know where I am going, but your other statement is at best hearsay and at worst, tittle-tattle."

The creature considered her words for a moment and then spoke. "Huzzah!," the creature said. "That may be true, but it seems that I am not the only one that is making assumptions. For you mistaken me for a flappy egg when it is clear that I am a penguin of the highest order."

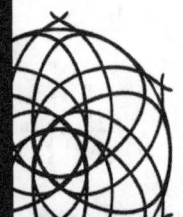
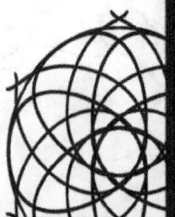

Kiko considered what the penguin had just said.

"Well then, Mister or Miss penguin," Kiko replied. "I apologize for my mistake. But I have also heard that a penguin is practically a chicken, and so you might be more of an egg than you think. Either way, I am looking for a nice patch of sunshine that I can lay down in and warm my belly. Is this such a place?"

The penguin flapped its featherless wings and burped.

"Yes and no," said the penguin. "For you see that there is much ice here and nothing more. It is true that there is also sunshine but it is not as warm as it appears. The ice is cold and the sun is warm. So, while you might get toasty on top, you will also get chilly on the bottom."

To Kiko this was unacceptable.

"My goodness!" she said. "A chilly bottom is the worst kind to have, besides a muddy one. This place is not going to be comfortable for me at all and so I must look elsewhere. I'll have to admit that I am quite disappointed because I was looking forward to learning some of your flappy ways. Where do you think I should look for my sunshine patch?"

"Well," the penguin said. "That I cannot tell you. But there is an underwater octopus that lives near the water's edge and she is very knowledgeable, especially about percussion instruments and accounting. Ask her, she might be able to help you. But beware, she is known to eat ice cream with a fork."

With that, Kiko walked toward the water's edge, hoping that the octopus had an answer for her.

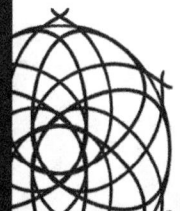
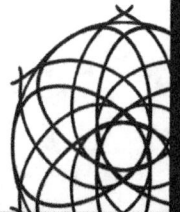

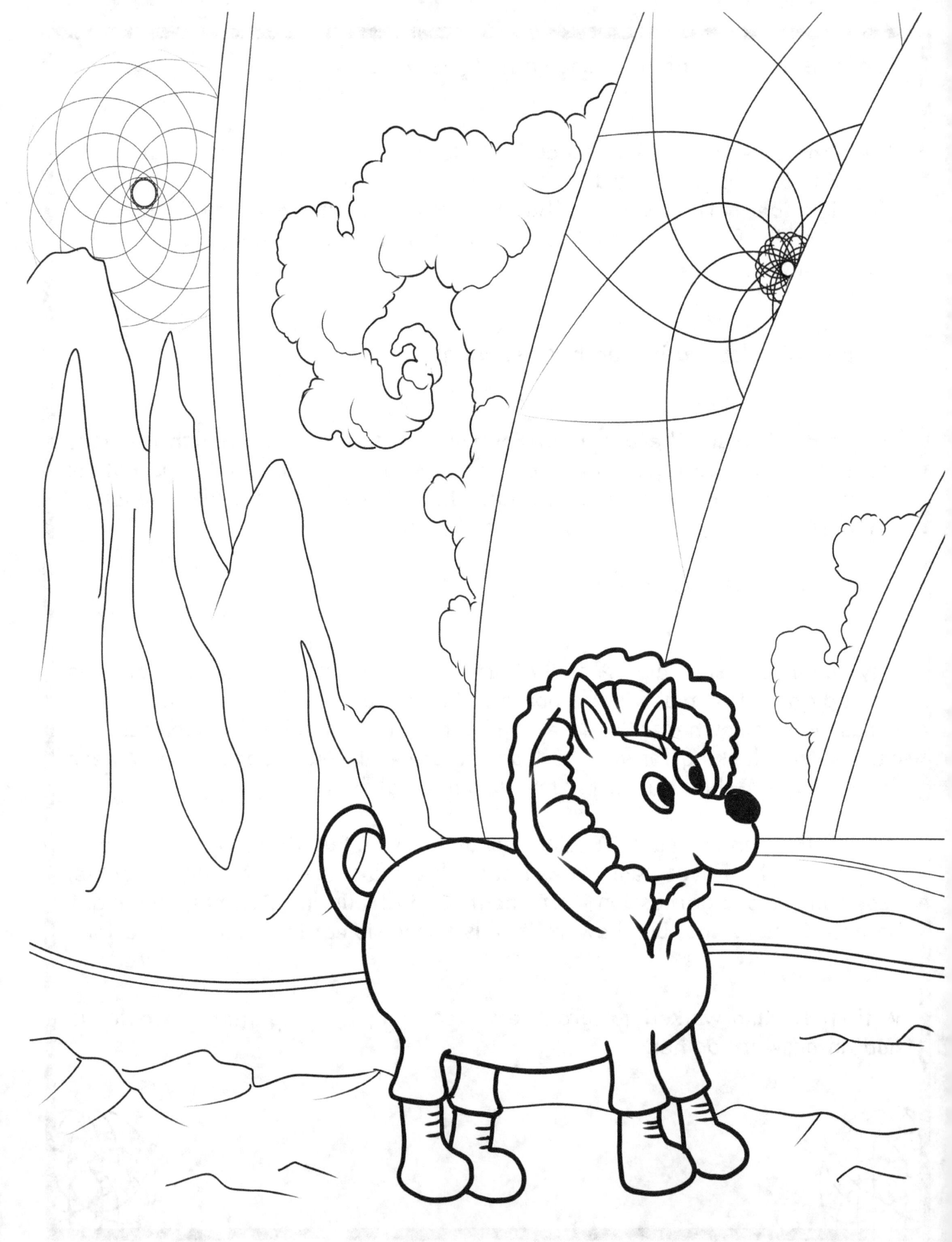

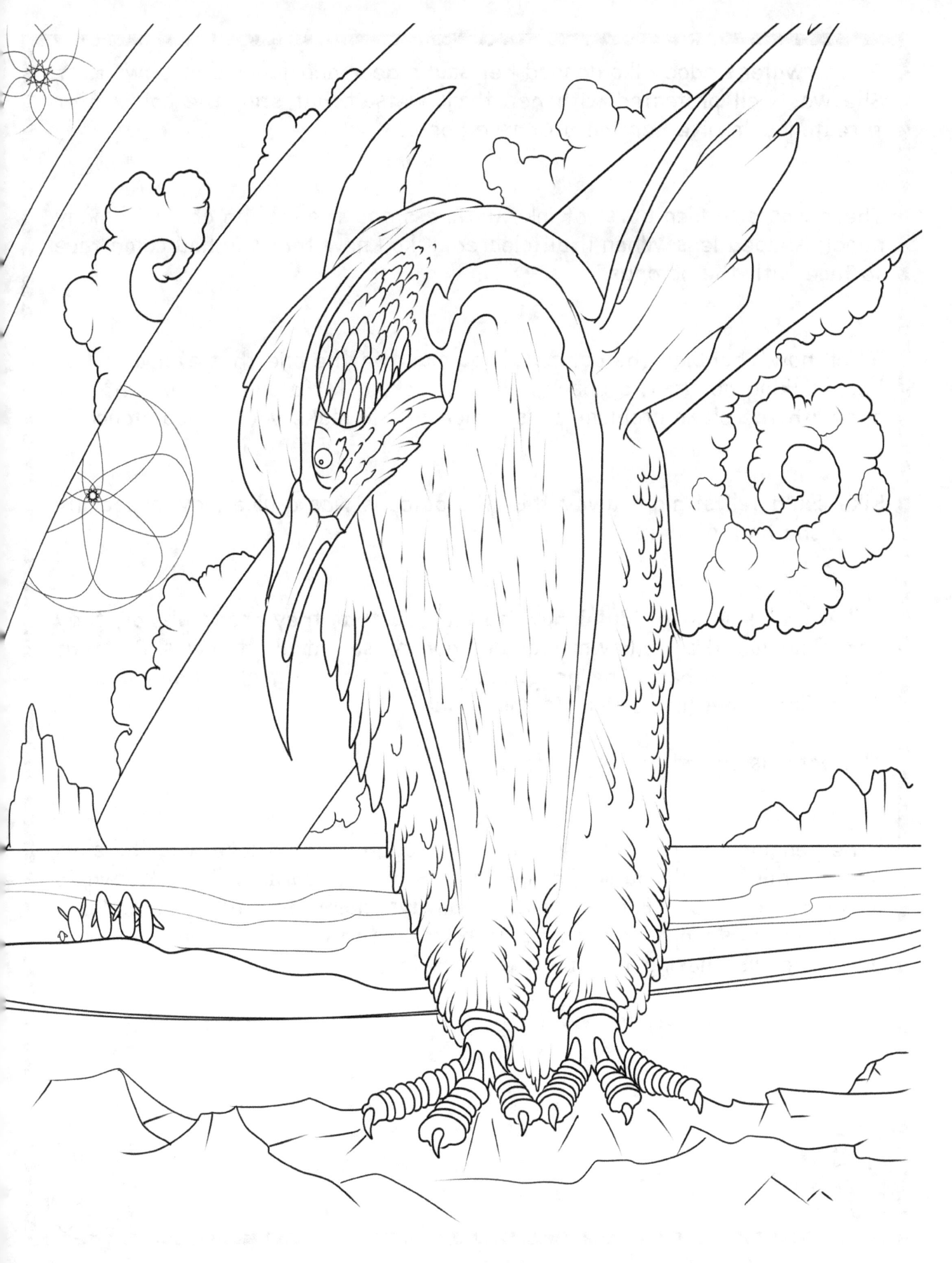

At the water's edge Kiko donned her scuba gear and jumped in, paws first. She was well protected with her thick wetsuit, but still, the cold water threatened to give her tail a Charlie horse.

There was a sudden burst of inky darkness and the moving about of many noodle shaped legs. When it all cleared, Kiko knew that she had come face to face with the octopus.

"Well now," bubbled the octopus. "You must be the one that everyone has been talking about: The basenji that is looking for a sunshine patch? The one with the pizza problem. It is a pleasure to make your acquaintance."

Kiko could tell straight away that the octopus was a nice lady, especially since she had manners.

"Likewise," said Kiko. "But I have to tell you that they aren't pizzas, they are mandalas, they follow me for no good reason at all, it seems. But that is not why I am here. The penguin told me that you might know where I could find a sunshine patch. Is this true?"

The octopus curled her legs into a ball.

"The penguin was correct," she said. "Although I would take what he says with a grain of salt. You see, despite his formal appearance, he is known to make bad decisions. For example, he always claims too many dependents and then cries when he has to pay extra at the end of the year. I would advise against making this mistake yourself."

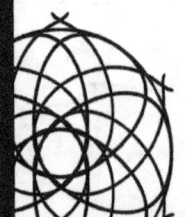
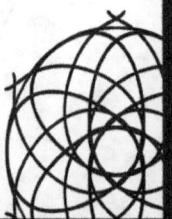

Kiko didn't make enough income to have to pay taxes, but she could see that the octopus was clearly frustrated having the penguin as a client.

"I will consider your advice should I become lawfully employed," said Kiko. "But getting back to the sunshine patch, is it anywhere around these parts?"

The octopus shook her bulbous head. "I am afraid that sunlight doesn't shine as much down in the water. So, you won't find such a place around here. I suggest that you take yourself back onto dry land and journey towards the East. That is where the sun lives."

Kiko cleared her snorkel.

"Thank you, Miss octopus," she said. "I will do just that. I think I feel a rash coming on from this wetsuit, anyway."

Kiko shook the octopus on the tentacle and slowly began to make her way to the surface.

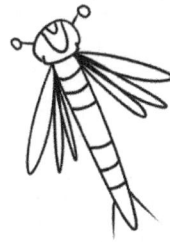

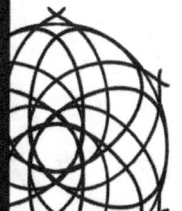
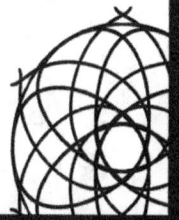

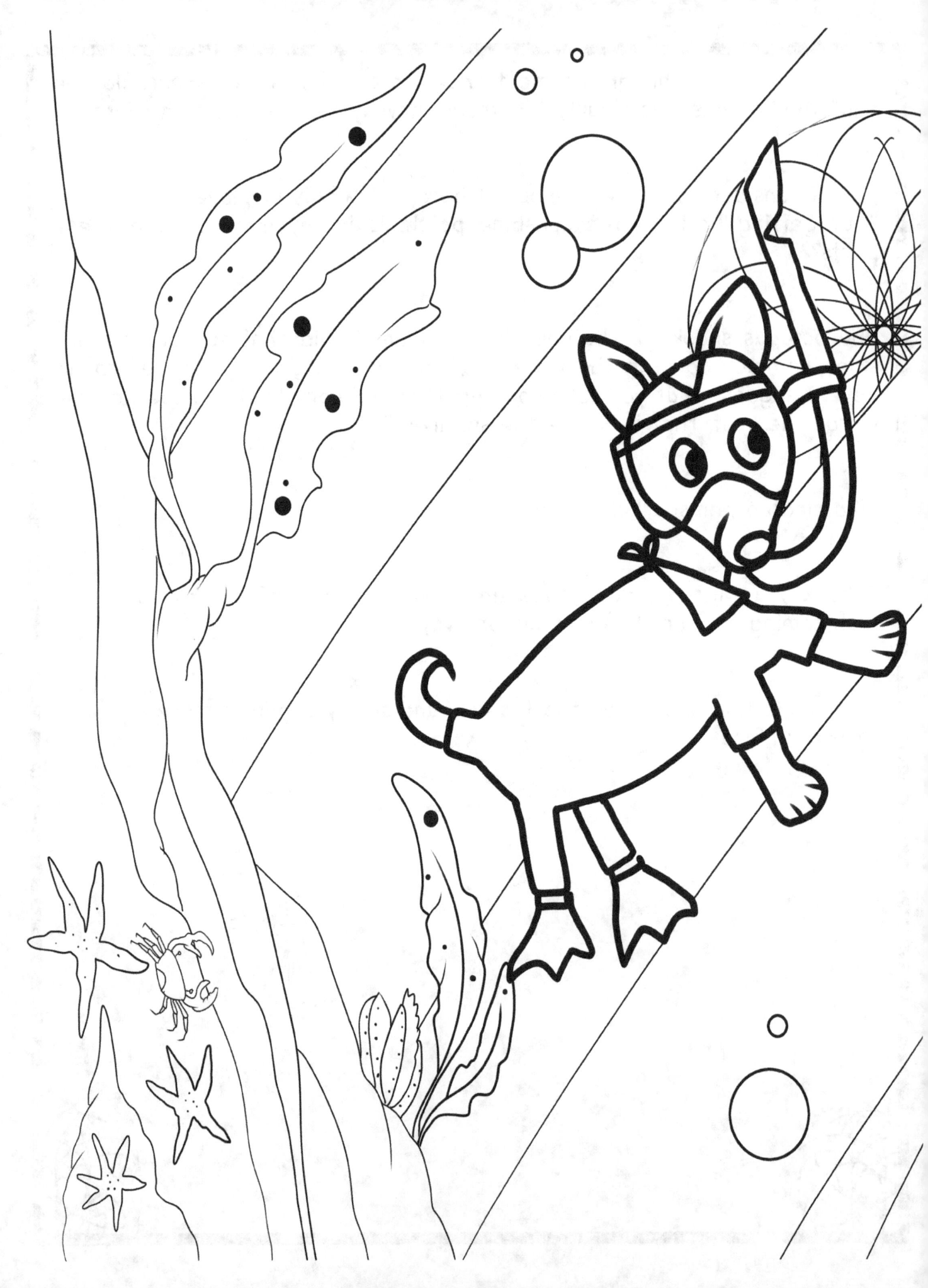

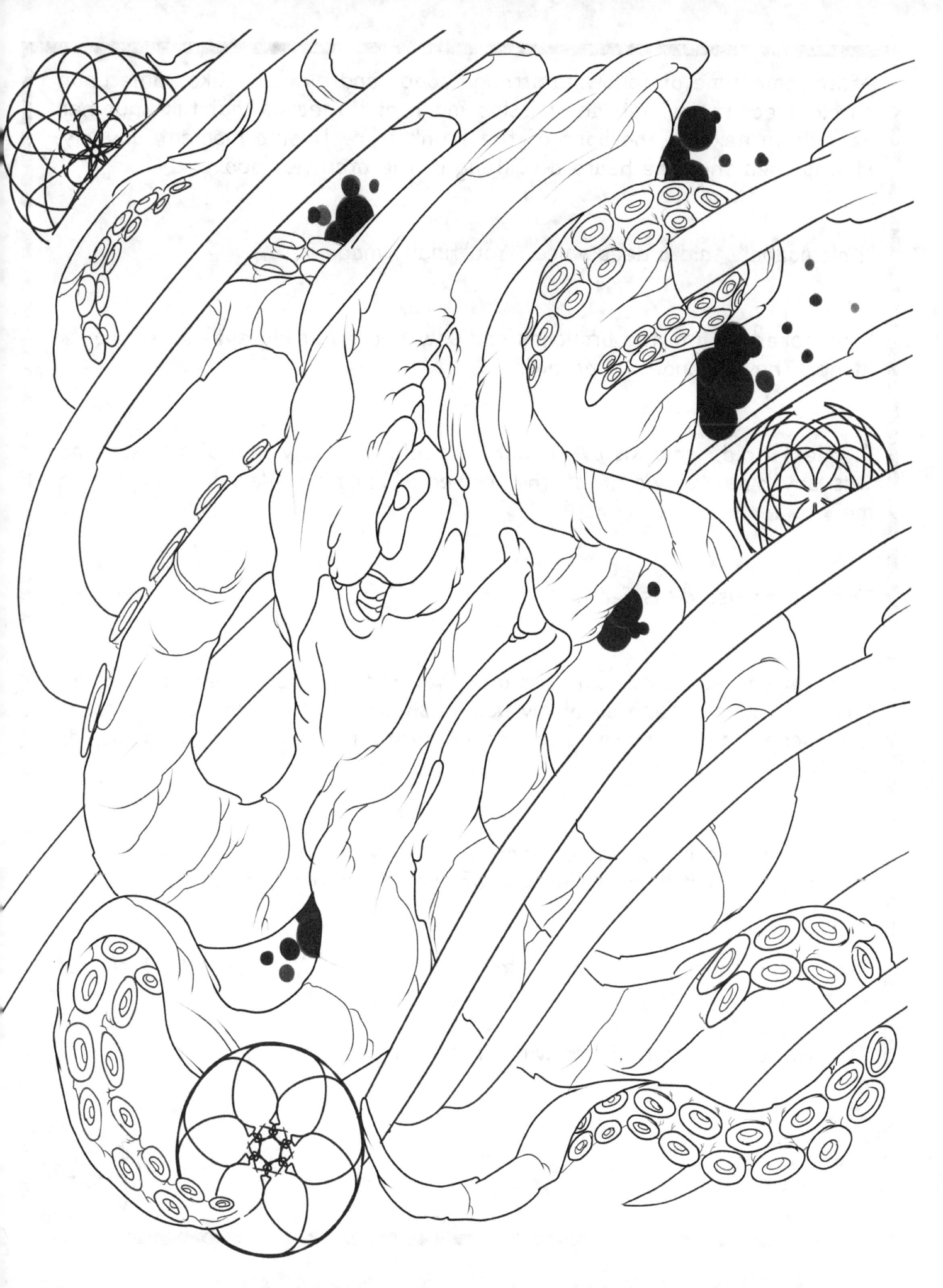

After some time of following strange roads and byways, Kiko came upon an old tree. It was tall and missing much of its leaves, but Kiko put her gear down next to the base of the trunk to rest for a moment, anyway. It was then that she heard a rustling in the branches above.

"Kalamazoo!" said a deep voice. "You finally made it!"

Kiko looked up into the branches and saw two great big eyes looking back at her. They belonged to an owl.

"I guess I did," said Kiko. Although she didn't see any sign of the sun and was anything but warm, at the moment. "I'm Kiko. Were you expecting me?"

The owl adjusted his feathery bottom.

"Well of course I was!" said the owl. "You are here to fix my wi-fi, aren't you? I've been missing all of my baking shows and have to make a croquembouche for an upcoming dinner party that I am hosting. Please, do whatever it takes to reset my router."

Kiko rummaged in her bag of gear for a router resetter but then realized that she had left it at the bottom of the sea with the octopus.

"I'm afraid that I have lost my tools," said Kiko. "Truth be told, I am not from the phone company, but am on a journey to the East to find the sun."

The owl looked down at her with unblinking yellow eyes.

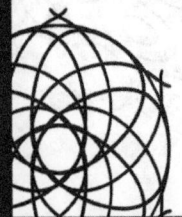
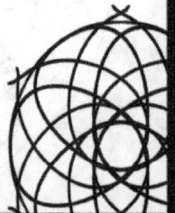

"Hmmpphh," he said. "That is really too bad. I am so tired of piggy backing off of my neighbor's signal. He is a kookaburra that lives in the tree over. He always resets his password and then I spend all night trying to hack it. It's really bothersome."

Kiko nodded. "Yes, I have heard that kookaburras can be very inflexible. But in regards to the sun, is it anyplace around here?"

The owl thought for a moment, the intensity of his gaze made Kiko feel like she was being examined by a pair of heat lamps.

"Now, the sun as you call it, does come out from time to time. In fact, you just missed it," the owl told her. "As far as that goes, you'll be chasing it for quite a while before you catch it. I suggest getting a hold of a big net. Preferably one made of titanium. That is, if you intend to get it to be still."

Kiko considered this for a moment. She had not thought about catching the sun and certainly didn't know where to find a net that big.

"You know, I think that I'll go on and keep looking for it," she finally said. "I don't know if catching it is such a good idea. After all, I just want to lay down and let it warm my belly."

"Well, you might be right about that," said the owl. "Your router resetting techniques leave much to be desired. Good luck little one."

And with that, Kiko continued on her journey.

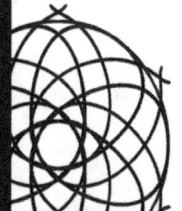
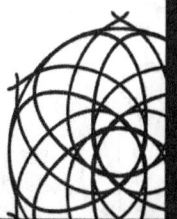

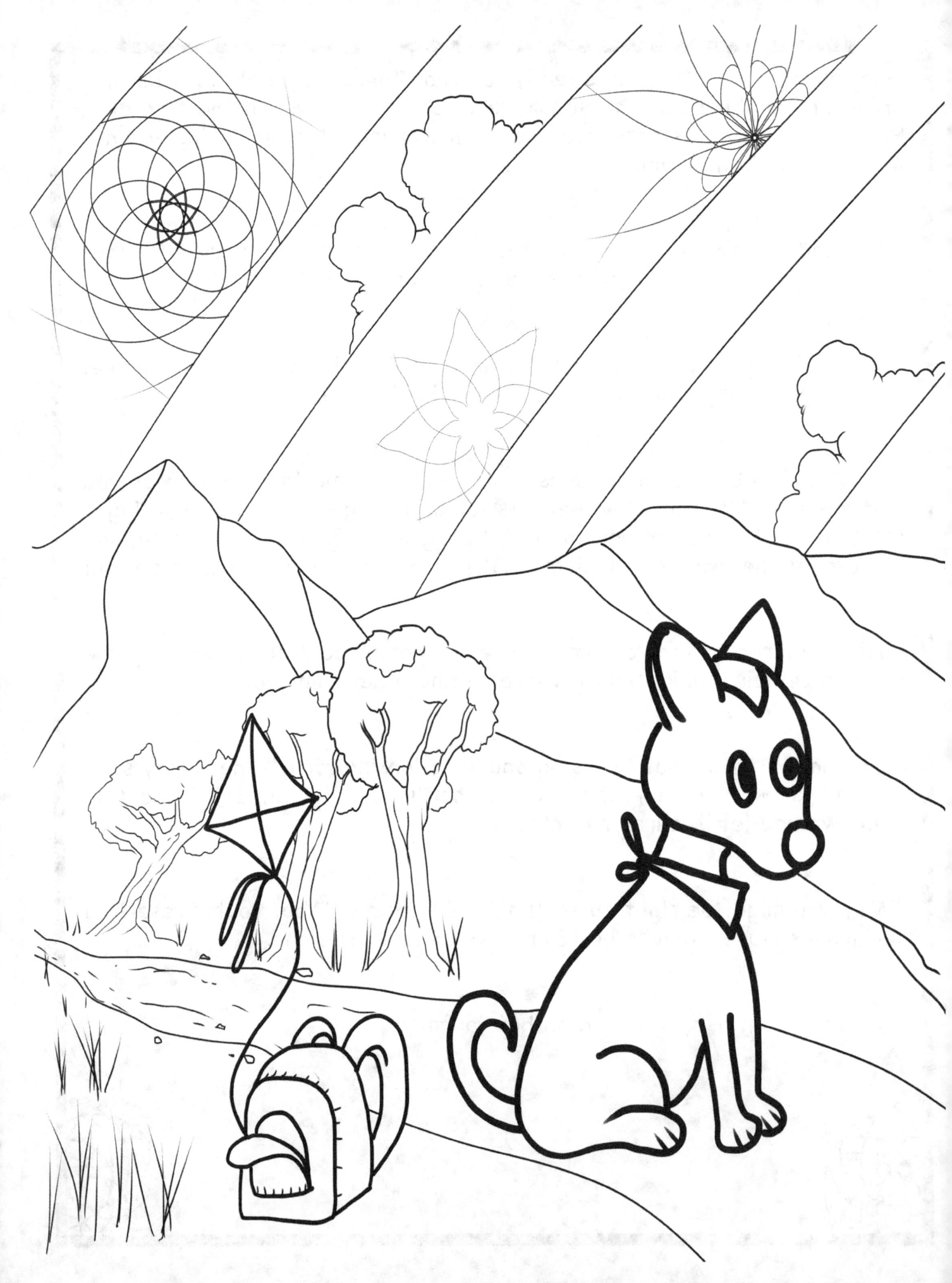

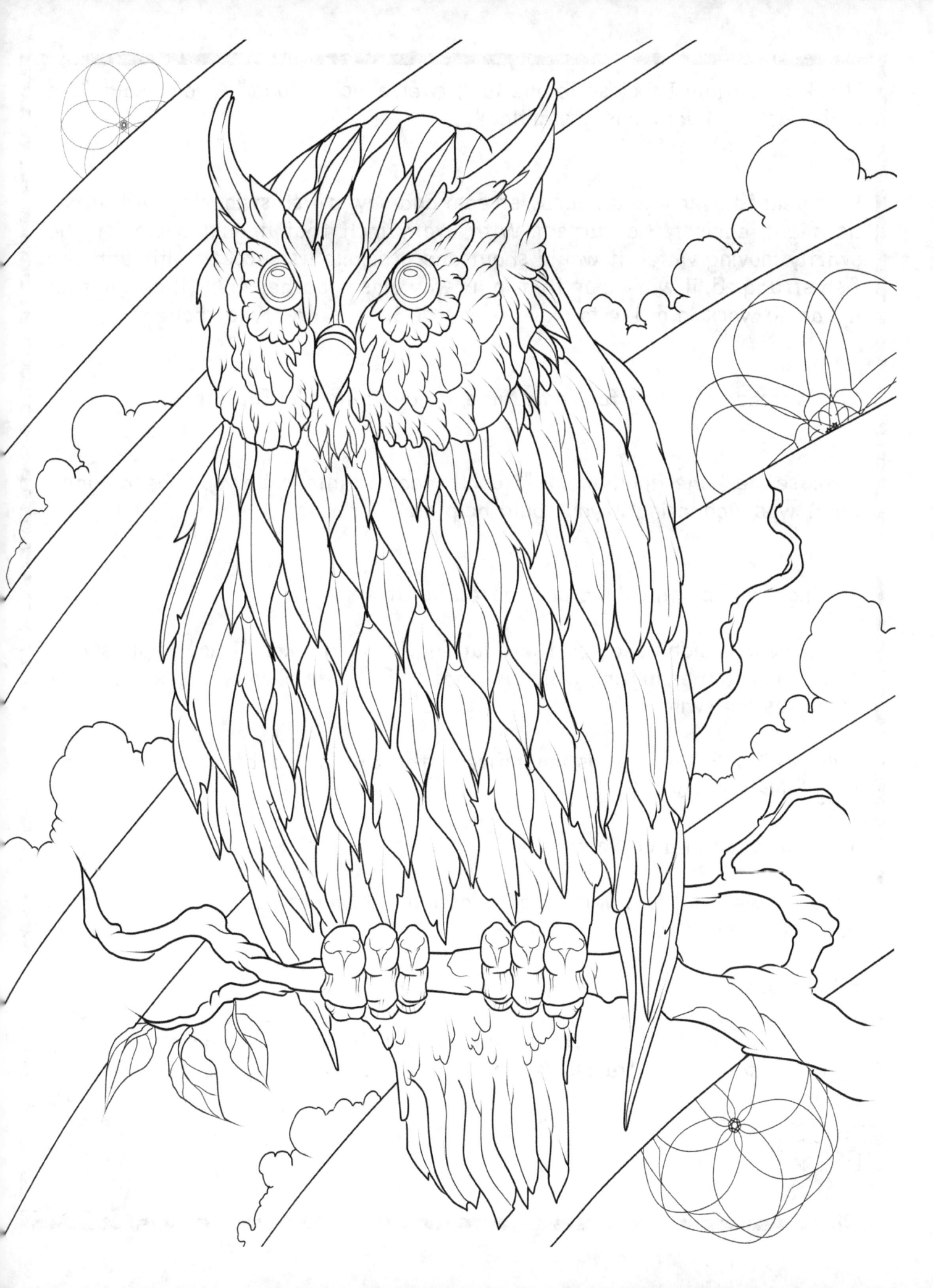

"Look at my tail! I'm close to one foot, twelve inches long!" A voice said. "I'm quite fast, and very easily startled!"

Kiko peered over into a nearby stream and saw a fish swimming with all of its might, against the current. With every inch that it gained amidst the swiftly moving water, it would shout and proclaim its success. Although the fish struggled, it was clear that in no way was it bothered by the fact that it had to work in order to move forward. Such is life, Kiko thought.

She watched the fish for some time, enjoying its playful antics.

"Excuse me," she finally said. "I don't mean to interrupt your shenanigans, but I was wondering if you could help me?"

The koi stopped thrashing and looked up at Kiko.

"Well hello, I didn't see you there lurking," said the koi. "I am simply swimming against the current, which is what I like to do. Have you seen my tail? It makes me swim quite fast."

"Oh yes," said Kiko. "It is magnificent, there is no doubt about that. How long have you had it?"

The koi swam in a circle to look at its tail.

"You known, that is a very good question," the koi said. "I suppose for as long as I can remember."

Kiko nodded.

"Yes, I have had mine for that long, as well," Kiko said. "I have seen many types of tails in my travels, but none as hard working as yours."

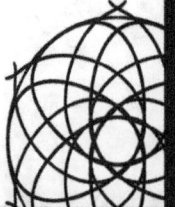

The koi splashed the water with his fins, he approved of her compliment.

"You are very wise for being so short," said the koi. "And I must say that I somewhat envy your pizza problem. Now, what can I help you with?"

"Well," Kiko said. "I have been on a journey to find a patch of sunshine that I can lay down in and warm my belly. But no matter where I go, I cannot seem to find it. I'm beginning to think that the sun doesn't like me much."

"Lasagna tacos!" said the koi. "That is simply untrue! I know the sun personally and I can say, without much uncertainty, that the sun loves everyone and everything. What you need to understand is that the sun is also very busy and is not much of a multi-tasker, so sometimes she can get distracted, especially during cheese rolling season."

Kiko knew that the koi was speaking the truth and his words made her feel better.

"I lost my watch going through airport security," said the koi. "But if I'm not mistaken, she should be visiting the garden very soon. You might want to check over there. Just watch out for the snake that lives in the flowers, he doesn't see so well and can be quite rude, especially if he hasn't had his coffee."

Kiko thanked the friendly koi, who then proceeded to swim hard against the current, splashing and singing his praises. She made her way toward the garden hoping to finally find some sun.

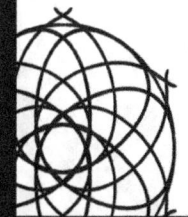
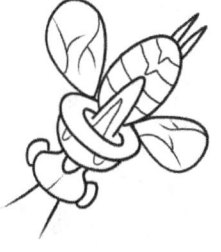
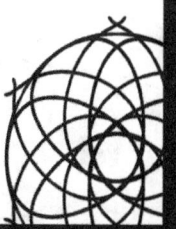

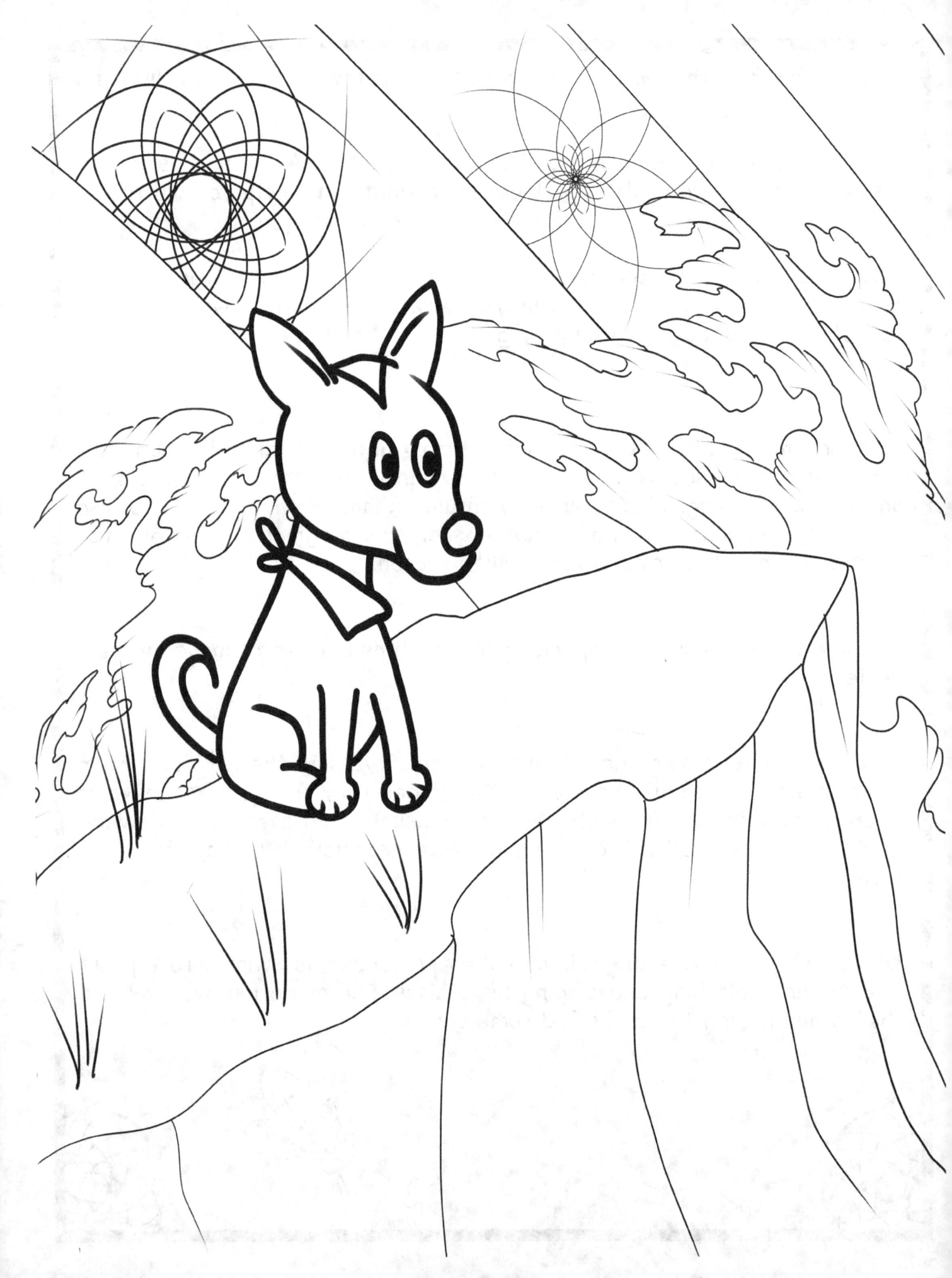

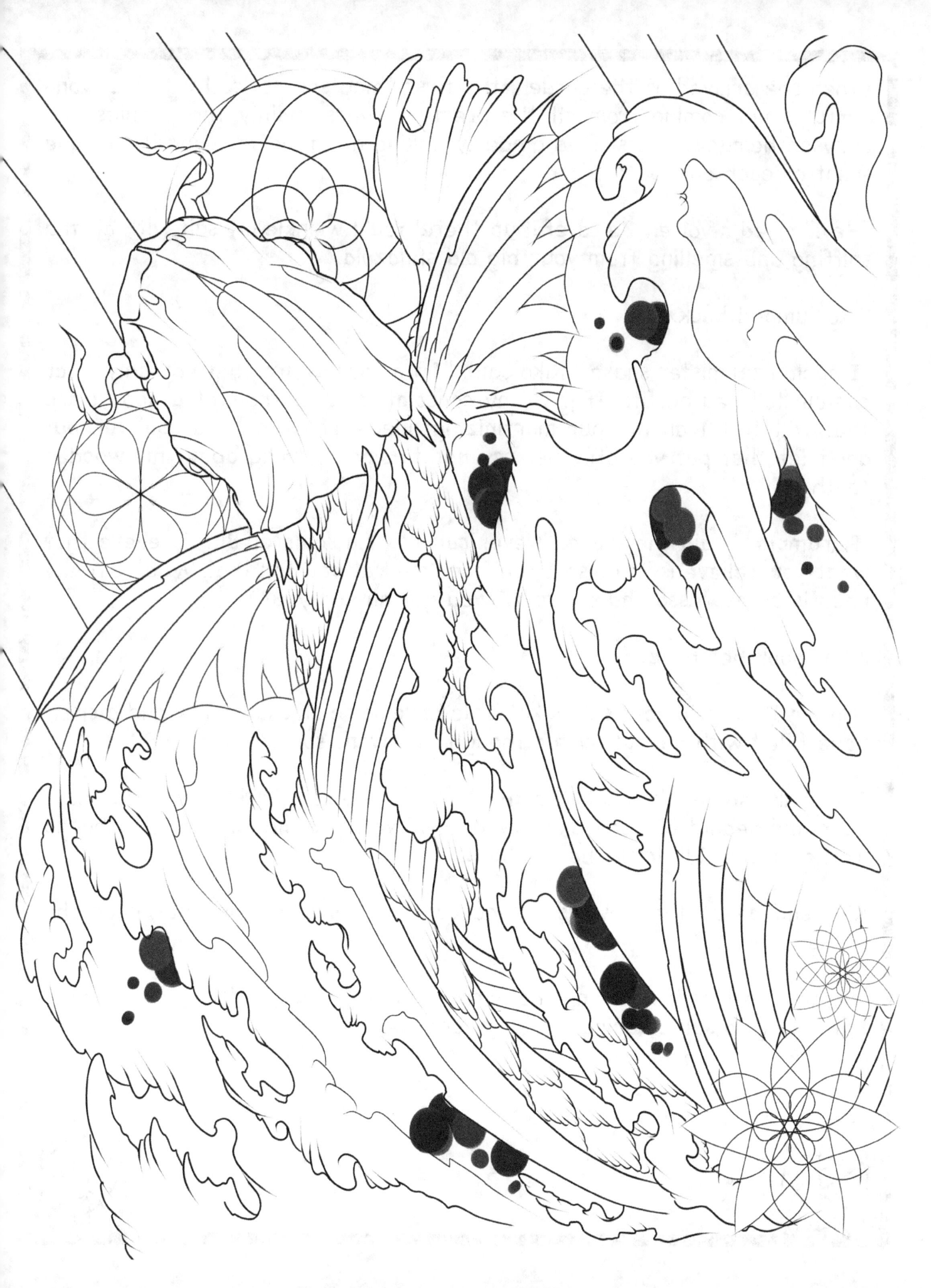

When she arrived at the garden, the first thing she noticed was the wonderful smell coming from all the pretty flowers, mainly the peonies and chrysanthemums. She sniffed gingerly, taking her time to savor the unique scent of each one.

"Hey!" cried a voice. "Be careful up there! You'll wrinkle my suit with all the sniffing and smelling from your big old shnazola."

Kiko jumped back.

"I apologize, mister snake," Kiko said. "I was not aware that you only wear custom tailored outfits. If it is any consolation, I do know of a good place that will fulfill all of your martinizing needs. It's run by a squirrel, but don't let that put you off. Just try not to say anything about his wooden teeth."

"Harumphh," said the snake. "Never can trust a squirrel. But I believe that what you believe is true, so I can't get mad at you for that. What I really need is an espresso and a biscotti. You got any on you?"

Kiko shook her head.

"No, sir, I'm afraid not," said Kiko. "I do have some chicken jerky and a chew bone filled with peanut butter though. You want some?"

The snake shook his head. "No thank you," he said. "Jerky gives me heart burn and peanut butter makes me gassy. I've got some left over kombucha in the 'fridge, I'll drink that for now."

Kiko sniffed at the flowers, taking care not to sniff the ones near the snake.

"So, what brings you around the garden, anyway?" asked the snake. "You're not trying to sell cleaning products, are you?"

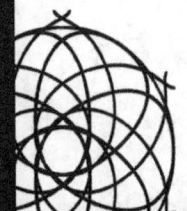
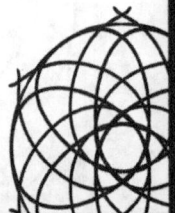

"No, not me," said Kiko. "I'm looking for a sunshine patch. The koi sent me over because he said that the sun might be here. I just want to lay down and let it warm my belly."

"Well now, ain't that a humdinger?" the snake said. "I too, like to warm my belly, it helps keep my quinsy from acting up. But I'll tell you what: that sun can be a real fickle pickle sometimes. She comes out one day, the next day she doesn't. It's enough to make you want to have a hissy fit."

"Well, I haven't had much luck finding her," Kiko said. "I've talked to frogs, cranes, whatever a foo dog is, a tiger, a penguin. Even an octopus and an owl. The koi told me to come see you because you're smart or something. If you can't help me then I might have to give up."

The snake snorted. "If I had a rattly tail I would shake it so hard, right now! I might be the best tailored animal you've ever seen, but I sure am not the smartest. If you're looking for smarts and wisdom, you need to go find the dragon. The dragon is the smartest and wisest of us all."

Kiko was excited now. "Well, tell me where the dragon lives so I can go straight away!", she said.

The snake coiled around some flowers and got comfortable.

"That's just the thing," said the snake. "The dragon doesn't really have a home, like we do. The dragon is a free spirit and likes to just show up and drop some wisdom on you. That's kinda his thing."

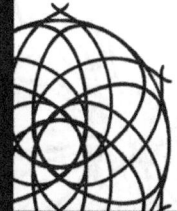
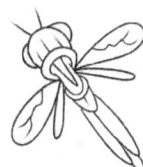
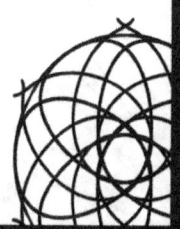

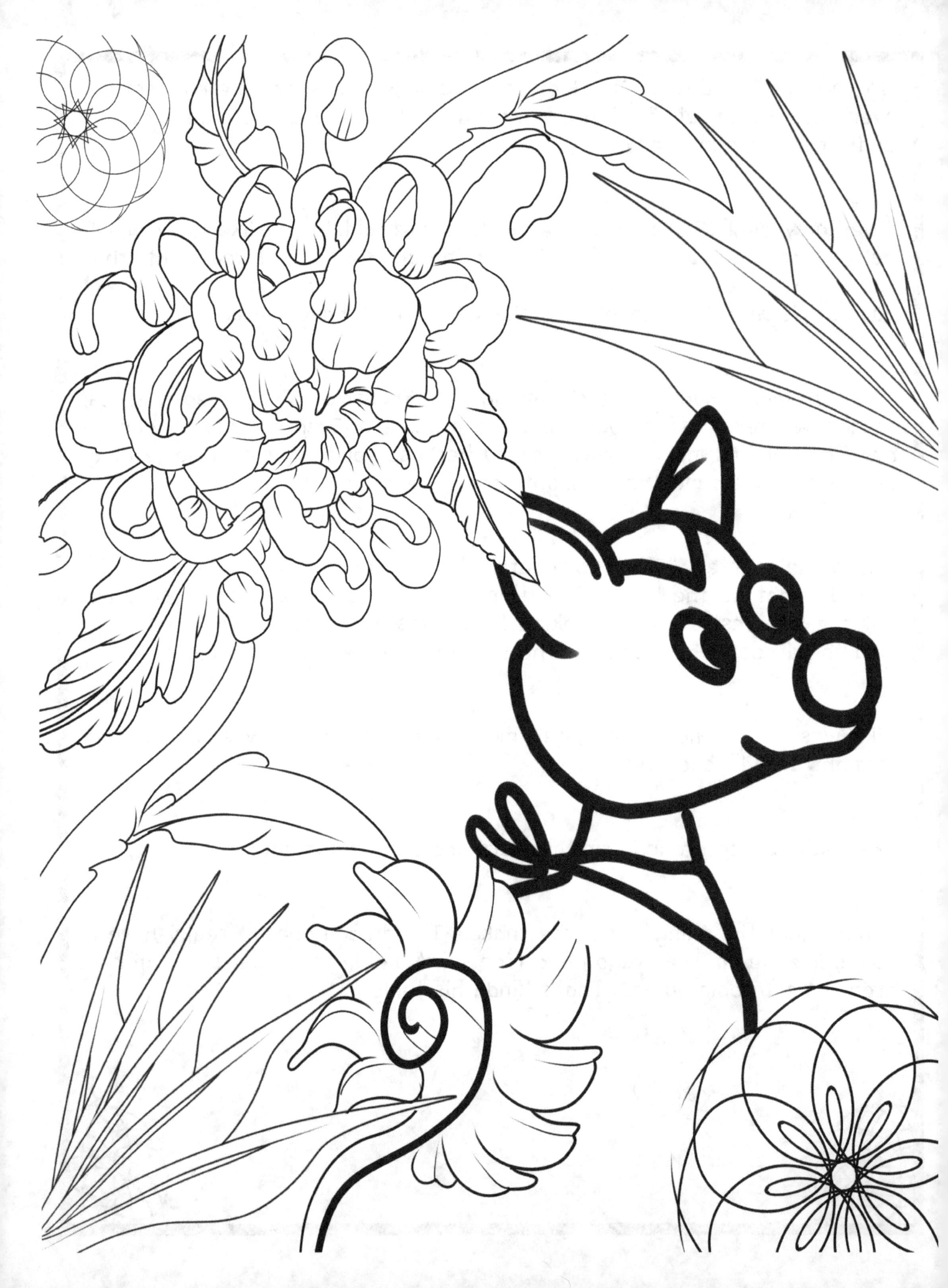

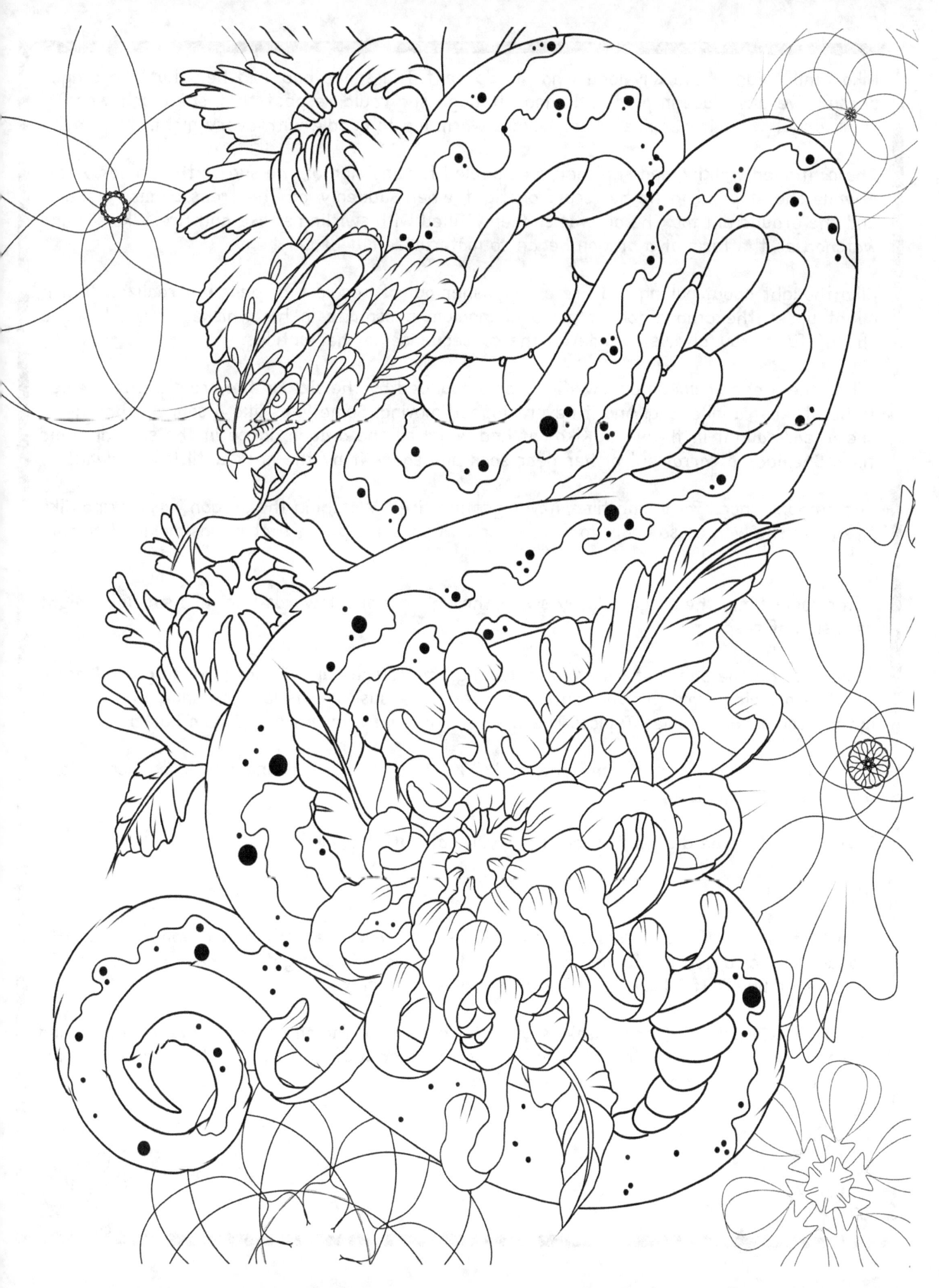

Kiko really didn't have any idea what to do next. The snake had told her that the dragon doesn't live any place in particular and although she could respect that, she didn't want to think about what it was like to not have a warm lap to cuddle with every night.

She continued walking and kept her eyes peeled for any sign of the sun or the dragon. After a while she stopped to tie her scarf on tight, when suddenly, all the trees began to shake, and the ground did too. The air was suddenly filled with swirling smoke and fire. Kiko sat and watched as the form of a dragon began to materialize out of mayhem.

Kiko thought about pulling the fire extinguisher out of her sack of gear but realized that it might upset the dragon to get mono ammonium phosphate in his whiskers. Kiko, being a thoughtful puppy, always considered the consequences of her actions.

When the dragon came into view, Kiko was astounded by the size of the creature. It seemed to be at least a mile long! And it never stopped moving. Sometimes like a snake, other times like a leaf caught in the wind. Kiko sat and watched the dragon dance in the sky for some time. She took a carrot out of her gear sack and shook it by the neck until it was dead.

The dragon danced for a long time, never getting tired. Watching the dragon was making Kiko tired and she wanted so badly to fall asleep in a sunshine patch that it was making her ears itch.

After some time, the dragon slowly swam through the sky towards her. Kiko sat up straight as a sign of respect.

"You must be the one that everyone is talking about? The puppy?" said the dragon. "I got a call this morning from the penguin and naturally, because it was long distance, he expected me to accept the charges. Typical. The wise never trust a bird dressed as a busboy."

Kiko nodded. "I am that puppy," she said. "But I rarely if ever dine out. And when I do, I always eat at the food court."

"Wise," replied the dragon. "Especially if you eat buffet style."

Kiko nodded.

"Now, let me see if I understand this correctly. You have been hither and yon, all over this wonderful world, looking for a sunshine patch. Is that about right?" asked the dragon. "To warm your belly? If I leave anything out, you let me know."

"No, I think you have it right," said Kiko. "I have traveled far and near, I have looked up and down, in the water and in the sky. And I haven't found a sunshine patch. Not one single one. I'm beginning to lose hope that I'll ever find it."

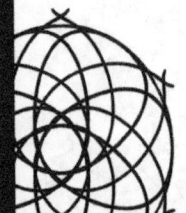
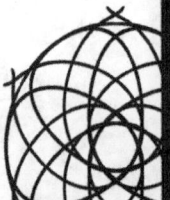

The dragon chuckled at what she said and then gave her a wink.

"Well, little basenji, consider this," said the dragon. "You have said that you traveled far and near, looked up and down and under the water. Talked to a frog, crane, foo dog, tiger, that tightwad the penguin, the octopus, the owl, the koi and finally the snake. And for all of that you find yourself here, with me. What if I told you that perhaps the sunshine patch isn't trying to avoid you as much as you are trying to find something that you had never lost. In fact, it has been with you for your entire journey."

The dragon looked quite content with himself. He preened his chin hair and stared off into the sky.

Kiko wasn't sure that she understood what the dragon was trying to tell her.

"Do you mean to tell me that the sun has always been with me and that somehow I didn't see it?" she asked. "I don't know if I am understanding you, I beg your pardon. Is this what wisdom is because I don't know if makes much sense to a puppy like me?"

The dragon belched out fire.

"Yes, this is wisdom or something very close to it," said the dragon. "Sometimes we look for things without, perhaps only to catch a fleeting glance of it from time to time, yet never do we possess it. But sometimes we need to simply look within, to find what we seek. It's quite simple, don't you see? Just so you know, I am very good at removing splinters and parsing contractual jargon, in case the need arises."

Kiko thought about it for a minute but she still couldn't wrap her head around the idea.

"If that is true," she said to the dragon. "Then why hasn't the sun come out? Why am I always missing it? If it was with me the entire time, then why would I be searching for it?"

The dragon let out a belly laugh and began to fade back into the smoke and fire.

"Exactly," he said. "Now you understand. Embrace your inner pizza problem. Keep your pleasant attitude and love for snacks with you always, little basenji. Never let them take your treats."

And with that the dragon disappeared into nothing.

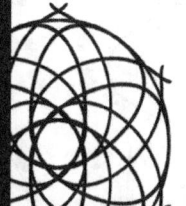
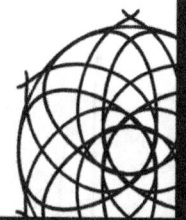

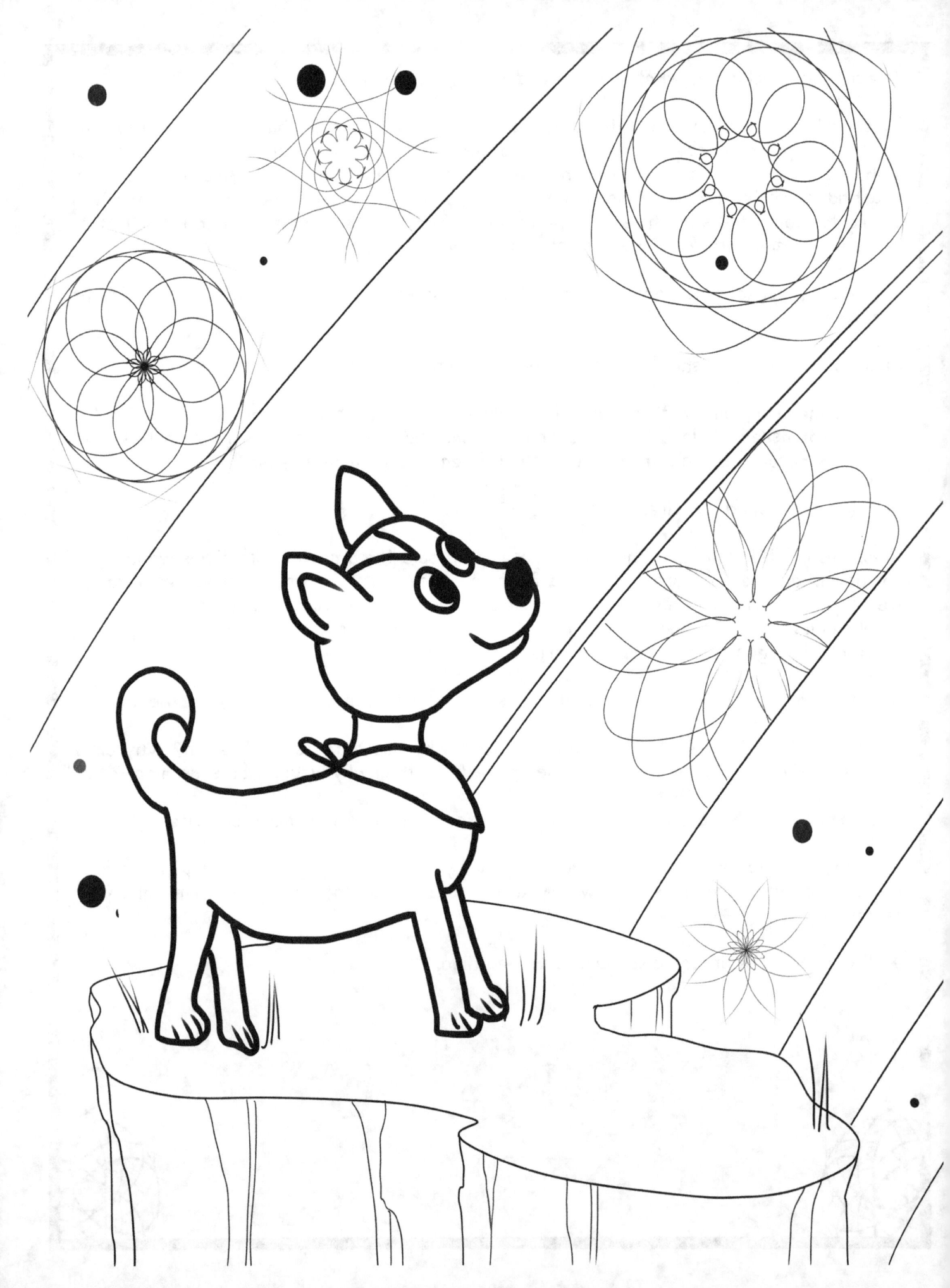

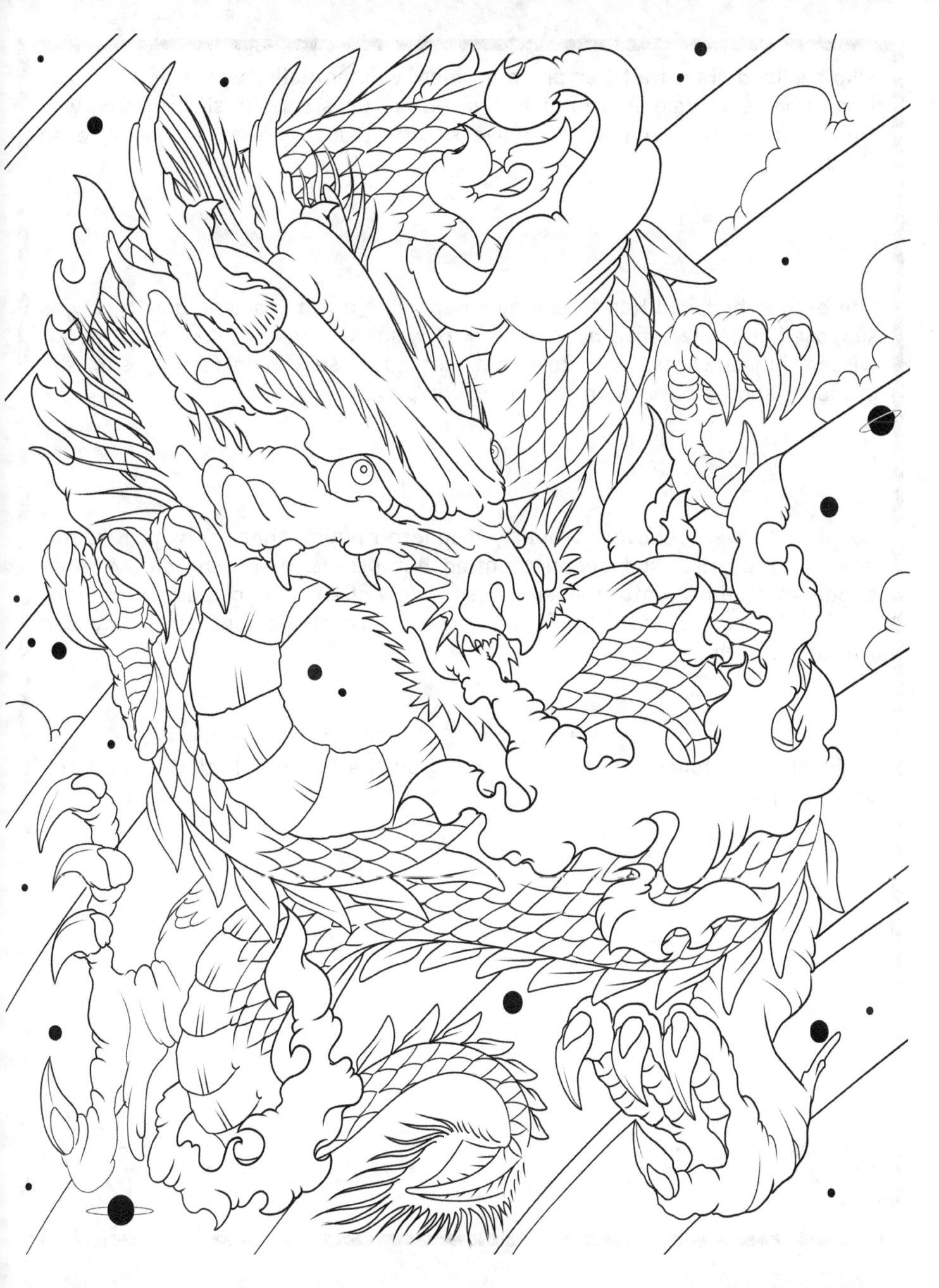

Kiko realized then that her pizza problem was actually a part of the solution. What she remembered of her world cultures class in sixth grade, was that mandala represented the universe, the place where we all live, even the sun.

The dragon had told her to embrace her inner pizza problem, and that was supposed to make sense because it was wise. Kiko didn't know much about wisdom but she was quite sure that instead of searching for the sun, she probably should have been searching for pizza.

So, like the well behaved, properly mannered puppy that she was, Kiko sat down in the grass and began counting her pizzas. While she did so, they began to multiply until the entire sky was filled with pizzas. They were beautiful, colorful and full of magic. They were also bright, and shiny and full of warmth.

Suddenly, Kiko found herself surrounded by the sunlight that she had been searching for all of this time.

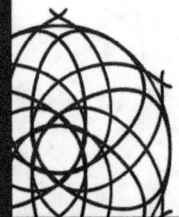

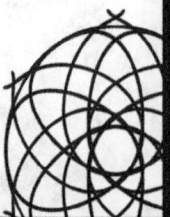

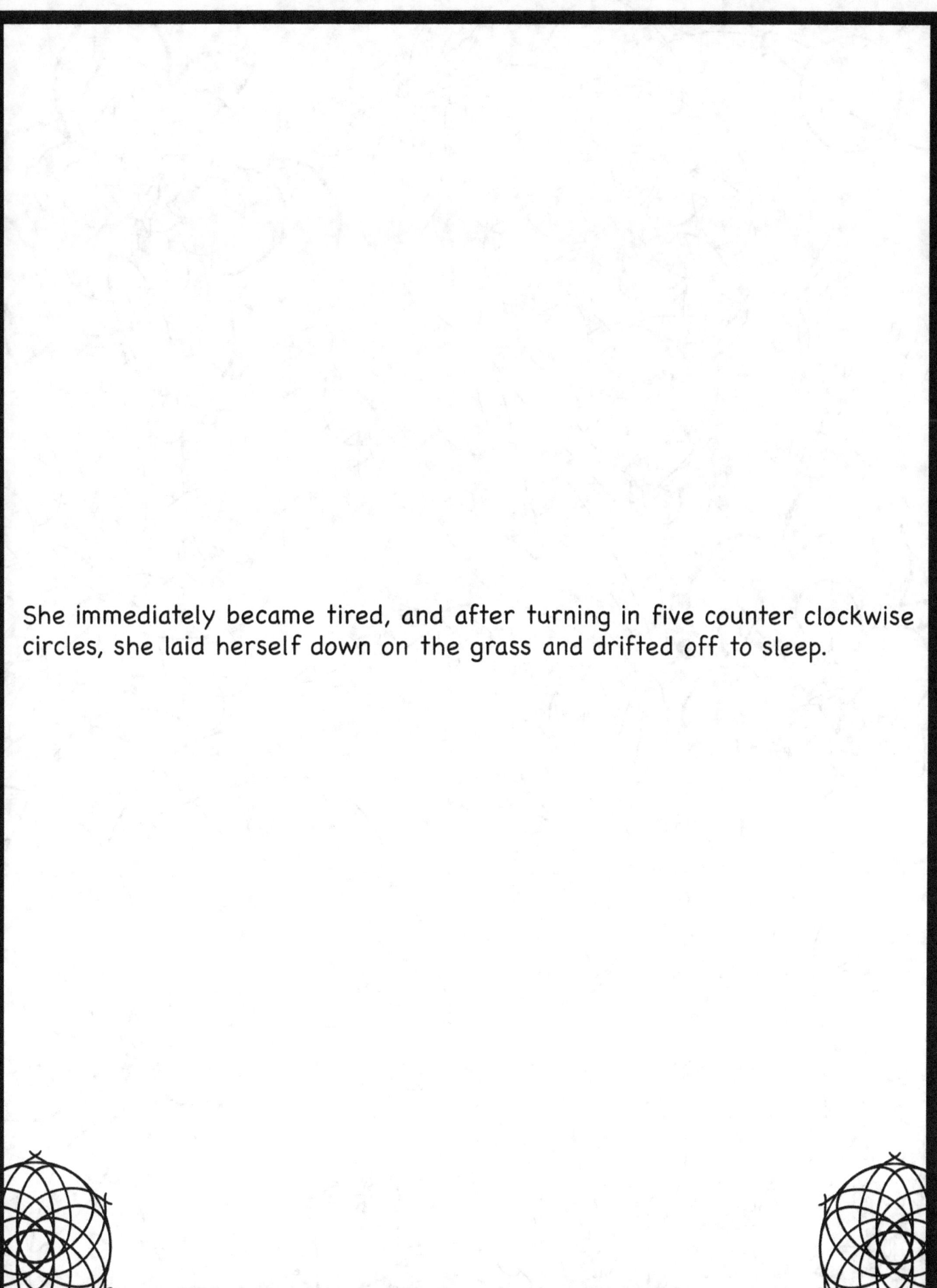

She immediately became tired, and after turning in five counter clockwise circles, she laid herself down on the grass and drifted off to sleep.

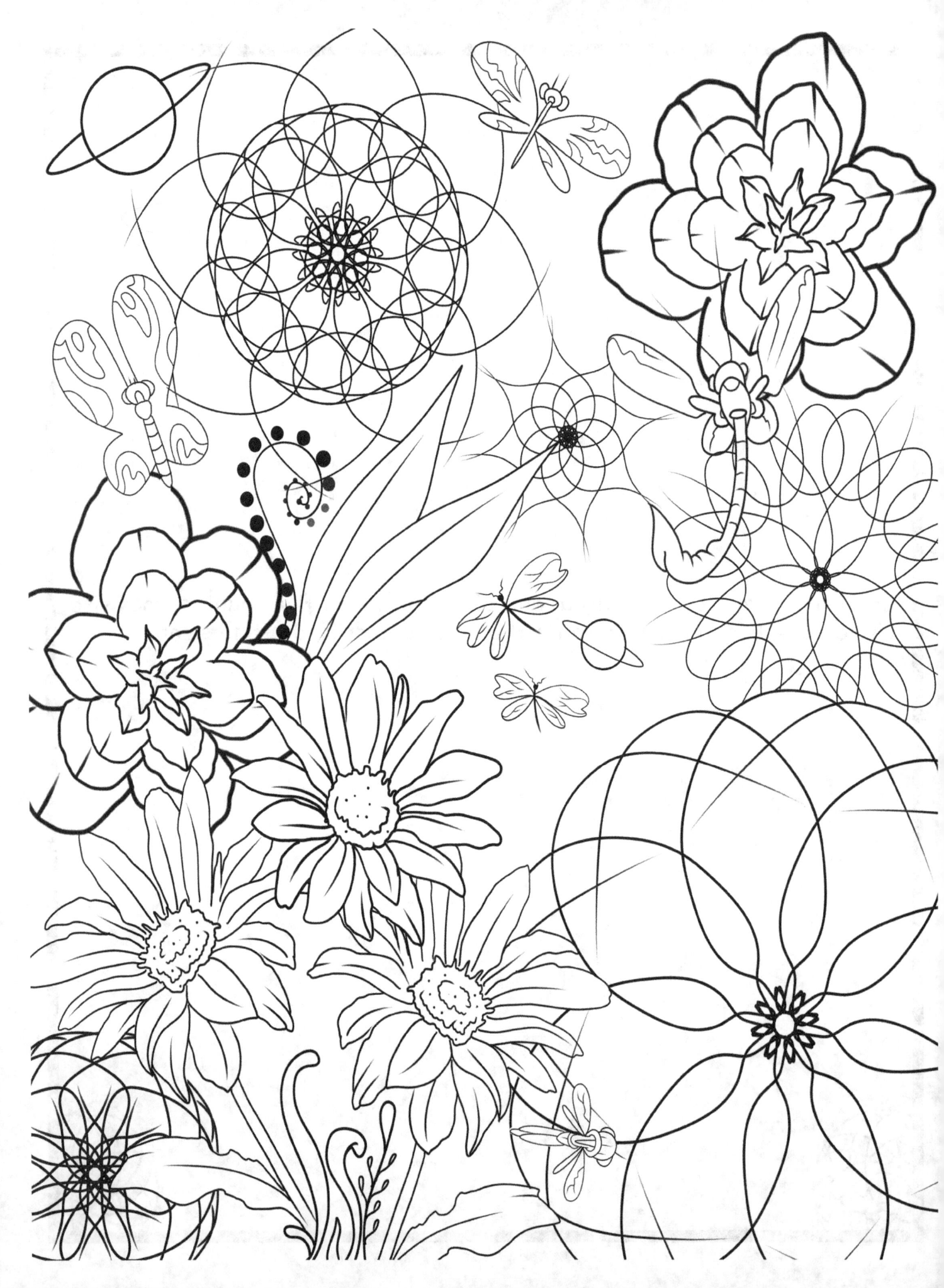

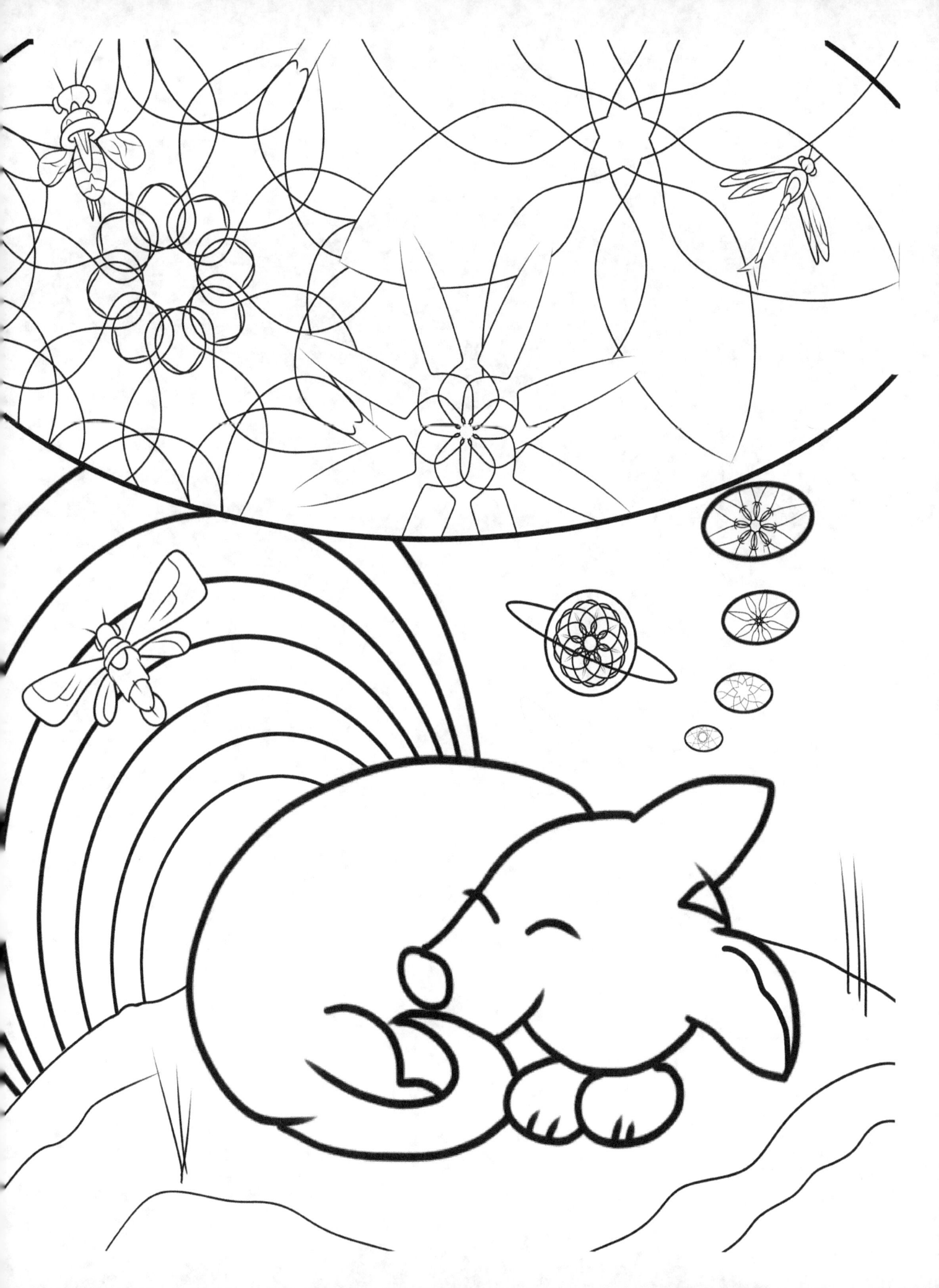